THE
EVERYTHING®

BABY NAMES
MINI BOOK

THE
EVERYTHING®

BABY NAMES
MINI BOOK

Traditional to original—
pick the perfect name!

Katina Z. Jones

Adams Media Corporation
Holbrook, Massachusetts

An Everything® Series Book.
Everything® is a registered trademark of Adams Media Corporation.

Published by Adams Media Corporation
260 Center Street, Holbrook, MA 02343
www.adamsmedia.com

ISBN: 1-58062-391-3

Printed in Canada.

J I H G F E D C B

Library of Congress Cataloging-in-Publication Data
available from the publisher.

Cover illustrations by Barry Littmann.
Interior illustrations by Barry Littmann and Kathie Kelleher.

*This book is available at quantity discounts for bulk purchases.
For information, call 1-800-872-5627.*

Contents

Introduction

Once upon a time, parents-to-be didn't think much about what they were going to name their babies. They figured they would either name their child after a favorite relative, or perhaps give him or her one of the names that were currently popular and that, more often than not, had religious origins.

Today, times have changed. Though there are still some parents who tend to pick a name out of a hat—or use the same name selection methods their parents and grandparents used—the majority of new parents today carefully consider a large variety of names before settling on one.

Why has this happened? Because we've changed. Even though a name is just a label we've put on a child in order to distinguish him or her from other children, a name is something to which people attach a lot of expectations and stereotypes, as much as we don't like to admit it.

Today, there are a wealth of names to choose from: the multicultural movement has popularized names from hundreds of ethnic groups, so you can select one that will be a first in your family; or you can choose a name that reflects on a well-loved relative; or you can even learn how to invent a name. Besides the fact that there have been many studies that indicate that the name a child bears—indeed, even an adult—has some influence on how he or she will be regarded by peers, the names you choose for your baby-to-be are the first links that you have to it. Once you choose a name for your girl or boy, you can begin to think of your baby in concrete ways, instead of just as an amorphous being that you'll get to meet a number of months down the road.

There are thousands of names to choose from in this book. Some of them are variations of a tried-and-true name, while others are so unique that a child who is given one of them might forever have to explain what it means or what his or her parents had in mind. But a lot of what's involved in bearing an unusual name revolves around attitude: many parents who bestow an uncommon name on a child are proud of the fact that their kid stands out, and will convey that attitude to their kid.

Should You Choose a Popular Name?

Throughout this book, you'll read about names that were popular for girls and boys during certain periods of time. Sometimes it's impossible to determine why a particular name was popular; frequently, it starts out as a snowball and gradually—or rapidly, in some cases—turns into an avalanche. For instance, Jennifer and Justin were around when I was growing up in the '60s, but they didn't make the top 10 name lists until the '80s, when they virtually exploded in popularity. But

now, while they're still around, they appear less frequently, replaced by Chelsea and Sophie for girls and Jordan and Dylan for boys. Sometimes, what makes a name become suddenly popular is that a public figure with the name becomes especially prominent.

The problem with giving your child a currently popular name is the chance that he or she will be in a class with four other kids who all have the same name. When I was growing up, I always thought it was a little bit sneaky when kids with the same names always ended up in different classes. But back then, the choices were

David, Robert, Laura, and Nancy—solid, untrendy names. Today, the more exotic names are, the more popular they are. But then again, David, Robert, Laura, and Nancy didn't appear on any most popular name lists prior to the '60s, so who knows—maybe the parents who chose these names were bucking tradition even back then.

But when a name is popular today, it means they are really popular. How much? Here's a breakdown: today, one out of every five girls has a name that falls into the top 10, while for boys, the figure jumps to one in three; one out of every two girls has a name that is in that year's list of top 50 names, while for boys, the frequency jumps to three in five.

Names and Stereotypes

One thing that you have absolutely no control over when choosing a name for your baby is the associations that other people will have with it. Think about that bratty kid in your third-grade class named Henry who teased you relentlessly. Be honest: today, whenever you meet someone with the same

name as a former tormentor, isn't there even the tiniest assumption that this new person has the same characteristics of the boy or girl who bugged you back then?

Similarly, some of the associations that we have with celebrity names can be just as damning—or complimentary, depending upon the name. In the late '70s, many parents rushed to name their daughters Farrah. When you meet one of these young women today named Farrah, what's the first thing you think of?

And the nature-oriented names that hippie parents christened their kids with back in the '60s through the mid-'70s today stand out. In the last year, I've met 20-somethings named Cinnamon and Charity. Of course, I didn't want to make a big deal out of their names, since they probably got this treatment all the time, but it was the name itself that initially cornered my thoughts, and not the person behind the name tag. Of course, after you get to know the person a bit, the initial surprise about the person's name tends to fade into the background. But keep in mind that some people are never able to get past *that name*, and therefore make instant assumptions about a person.

But then again, a name doesn't have to belong to a celebrity or serve as a barometer of the social times to provide people with a stereotyped image of the person behind the name. Some names just have a certain sound to them that helps paint a picture in our minds. Just try to imagine the different physical characteristics you would expect the following names to embody: Bertha, Blythe, Chloe, Gladys.

Americans frequently say they eschew labels, but in the end, slapping a label—or in this case, a name—on things or people before you get a chance to become familiar with them is the brain's natural way to make sense of something new. Unfairly, certain names also help us to decide whether to spend the time to know more about that person.

In quieter, more personable times, a name was an expression of virtue. During the 1800s, names such as Patience, Prudence, and yes, Chastity and Charity embodied traits to strive for. And yet, these and other names specific to a particular decade or century are in themselves labels. Think about it: what did a rebellious teenager in Victorian times do with a name like Prudence if she clearly wasn't prudent? The fact that she was christened with this very name might have encouraged the adults around her to become more impatient with her if it was clear that she wasn't anything like her name.

Today, those big blue "hi-my-name-is" tags tell a whole lot more about you to the world than you really want. So take some time to think about what you'd like your child's name tag to convey to the world.

How to Use This Book

Today, we all hear stories about the parents who put their children on waiting lists for the top private kindergartens—when these kids haven't even been born yet. As we are a nation of people who ponder every move for how it will affect us in the future, our concerns for our soon-to-be-born children fall along the same lines. You can read about the kind of music to listen to, the foods you should eat during pregnancy to ensure a larger-than-

normal brain in your baby, and even the type of work and leisure activities you should undertake in order to keep your baby calm both before and after it is born.

As you thumb through the listings, circle the names that seem like possibilities to you, and try to imagine your child outside playing while you call him or her in to dinner. How will it sound?

Then, imagine your child as an adolescent, with all the joys and terrors that this implies. No matter what name you give your baby, whether common or unusual, you should know now that your teenager will probably hold it against you in some way because the coolest kid in her grade has a

name that is either more traditional or more unusual. You can't win.

But then, picture your baby as an adult with kids of his own. What does his wife call him? And does your grown child fit the name you gave him so many years ago?

A name is such a personal thing that it makes sense to spend some time making the all-important decision of what to call your new baby. This book will help you to make this momentous choice.

Boys' Names

A

AARON (Hebrew) Lofty or exalted. The older brother of Moses, appointed by God to be his brother's keeper. Aaron has actually been one of the more popular names since the early days of the United States in the 1600s. Famous people from the past and present with the name include a vice president, Aaron Burr, the American composer Aaron Copland, and the singer Aaron Neville. Variations: *Aarao, Aharon, Arek, Aron, Aronek, Aronne, Aronos, Arran, Arren, Arrin, Arron.*

ABDUL (Arabic) Servant.

ABDULLAH (Arabic) Servant of God. Variation: *Abdulla*.

ABEL (Hebrew) Breathing spirit or breath. In the Bible, Abel was the second son of Adam.

ABID (Arabic) One who worships Allah. Variation: *Abbud*.

ABNER (Hebrew) Father of light. Biblical. Variations: Aviner, Avner.

ABRAHAM (Hebrew) Father of many. If the name Abraham conjures up an image of a wise old man to you, you may scoff at the idea of making an infant put up with the name until it fits, say, oh, in 60 years or so. But as more and more parents decide to give their children names that conjure up American history, Abraham will continue to have a growing place in baby names. Variations: *Abe, Abrahamo, Abrahan, Abram, Abramo, Abran, Abrao, Avraham, Avram, Avrum*.

ACE (English) Unity. Nickname given to one who excels.

ACTON (English) Town in Great Britain.

ADAM (Hebrew) Man of the red earth.
Adam was the first man who made it
into the world, and his name has
always been popular in many coun-
tries and in many religions. Many
parents pick the name for their first son.
Variations: *Adamec, Adamek, Adamh, Adamik,*
Adamka, Adamko, Adams, Adamson, Adamsson,
Adan, Adao, Addam, Addams, Addamson, Addie,
Addis, Addy, Adhamh, Adnet, Adnot.

ADDISON (English) Son of Adam.

ADISA (African: Nigerian) One who is clear.

ADOLPH (German) Noble wolf. Variations: *Adolf,*
Adolfo, Adolphe.

ADRIAN (Latin) Black; dark. Variations: *Adrean, Adren.*

AHMAD (Arabic) More deserving. Variation: *Ahmed.*

AHMED (Arabic) Praise. Variation: *Ahmad.*

AIDAN (Irish, Gaelic) Warm. Aidan is the name of an Irish saint from the year 600 A.D.

AJANI (African: Nigerian) He fights for possession.

AKAMU (Hawaiian) Red earth. Variation: *Adamu.*

AKIM (Russian) God.

ALAN (English, Celtic) Fair; handsome. If you want a steadfast name that will stand out, Alan is a good choice. Variations: A*ilean, Ailin, Al, Alain, Aland, Alano, Alanson, Alao, Alen, Alin, Allan, Allayne, Allen, Alleyn, Alleyne, Allin, Allon, Allyn, Alon, Alun.*

ALBERT (Old English) Bright; brilliant. Variations: *Alberto, Albie, Albin, Albrecht.*

ALDRICH (English) An old and wise leader.

ALEXANDER (Greek) Protector; helper and defender of mankind. Alexander is one of those great, strong names that stands well on its own as well as in one of its many versions. Variations: *Alasdair, Alastair, Alaster, Alec, Alejandro, Alejo, Alek, Alekos, Aleksander, Aleksandr, Alesandro, Alessandre, Alessandri, Alessandro, Alex, Alexandre, Alexandro, Alexandros, Alexei, Alexi, Alexio, Alik, Alisander, Alissander, Alissandre, Alistair, Alister, Alistir, Allistair, Allister, Allistir, Alsandair, Alsandare, Sacha, Sande, Sander, Sanders, Sanderson, Sandey, Sandie, Sandor, Sandy, Sascha, Sasha, Sashenka, Sashka (Russian), Saunders, Saunderson.*

ALI (Arabic) Elevated.

ALPHONSE (German) One who is ready to fight. Variations: *Alfonse, Alfonso, Alfonze, Alfonzo, Alonzo, Alphonso.*

ALTAIR (Greek) Bird.

ANDRE (French) Manly. French version of Andrew. Variations: *Ahndray, Andrae, Andray, Aundray.*

ANDREW (English) Manly; brave. Andrew has always been a popular name for boys in this century, not only in English but in many languages. The

name Andrew conjures up both dignity and infor-
mality, traits that served United States Presidents
Andrew Johnson and Andrew Jackson. Variations:
*Aindrea, Aindreas, Anders, Andi, Andonis, Andor,
Andre, Andreas, Andrei, Andres, Andrey, Andy.*

ANGELO (Italian, Portuguese, Spanish) Messenger;
angel. Variation: *Angel.*

ANTHONY (Latin) Praiseworthy; valuable. Saint
Anthony is the patron saint for poor people.
Variations: *Andonios, Andonis, Anntoin, Antin,
Antoine, Anton, Antone, Antonello, Antoney,
Antoni, Antonin, Antonino, Antonio, Antonius,
Antons, Antony, Antos.*

ARLO (Spanish) Bayberry tree. Even though the only
Arlo you may have heard of is Arlo Guthrie, the
name is actually a common Italian version of
Charles.

ASHER (Hebrew) Happy. Asher was one of Jacob's
sons in the Bible. The ash tree supposedly brings
good luck; one belief is that if you give a bit of sap
from an ash tree to an infant, he will be lucky the

rest of his days. Variations: *Anschel, Anshel, Anshil, Ashu.*

AUSTIN (English) Majestic. Austin, along with its variants, is currently one of the more popular names. Especially with the recent newfound popularity of writer Jane Austen, this name seems to be at the forefront of an explosion in "veddy British" names on these shores. Austin has recently held the honor of being the most popular name for newborn boys in a few of the western United States. Famous Austins are still few and far between, until those in the current crop hit their stride. Variations: *Austen, Austyn.*

AVERY (English) Counselor. This name fits tidily into the trend of naming a baby after a town or place, and also as an androgynous name that suits both boys and girls equally well.

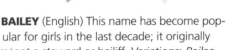

BAILEY (English) This name has become popular for girls in the last decade; it originally meant a steward or bailiff. Variations: *Bailee, Bailie, Baillie, Baily, Baylee, Bayley, Bayly.*

BALDWIN (German) Brave friend. Variations: *Bald, Baldovino, Balduin, Baldwinn, Baldwyn, Baldwynn, Balldwin, Baudoin.*

BARRY (Gaelic) Pointed object. Barry is also increasingly being used as a girls' name with the spelling of Barrie. The name, however, is not as popular as it was a couple of decades ago. Variation: *Barrymore.*

BARTHOLOMEW (English) Farmer's son. There are countless derivatives that come from Bartholomew, which was the name of one of the 12 apostles. Today, the most famous celebrity who goes by a shortened version of Bartholomew is none other than Bart Simpson. Variations: *Bart, Bartel, Barth, Barthel , Barthelemy , Barthelmy, Barthlomeo, Bartholome, Bartholomieu, Bartlett, Bartoli, Bartolo, Bartolomeo, Bartram.*

BARTON (English) Field of barley.

BEAU (French) Beautiful. Variation: *Bo*.

BENJAMIN (English) In the Bible Benjamin was the youngest son of Jacob. The name translates to son of my right hand. The name Benjamin has become extremely popular in recent years, but it has been a great American staple since the days of Benjamin Franklin. Variations: *Benejamen, Beniamino, Benjaman, Benjamen, Benjamino, Benjamon, Benji, Benjie, Benjiman, Benjimen, Benjy, Bennie, Benny, Minyamin, Minyomei, Minyomi*.

BENSON (English) Son of Ben. Last name. Variations: *Bensen, Benssen, Bensson*.

BERNARD (German) Brave. Bernard has a long and illustrious history. Two saints from medieval days went by the name of Bernard, as does the heroic dog considered the patron saint for hikers. Variations: *Barnard, Barnardo, Barney, Barnhard, Barnhardo, Barnie, Barny, Bernardas, Bernardel, Bernardin, Bernardino, Bernardo, Bernardyn, Bernhard, Bernhardo, Bernie, Berny, Burnard*.

BEVAN (Welsh) Son of Evan. Its usage today is becoming more popular. Variations: *Beavan, Beaven, Beven, Bevin, Bevon.*

BILL (English) Bill is rarely a given first name. It is a variation of the more formal name William, which most parents of "Bills" choose to name their boys. Variations: *Billy, Byll.*

BLAKE (English) This name could be given to both boys and girls, and strangely enough, could mean either light or dark. Variations: *Blaike, Blayke.*

BOYD (Gaelic) Blonde. Variation: *Boid.*

BRADLEY (English) A wide meadow. Bradley is one of those names that seems to always skirt the edge between extreme popularity and obsolescence. In the '70s, it seemed like a slightly nerdy name but was saved by the virile sound of its nickname: *Brad.* Undoubtedly, its growing popularity is due to the fame of the movie star Brad Pitt. Variations: *Brad, Bradlea, Bradlee, Bradleigh, Bradlie, Bradly.*

BRADY (English) Wide island.

BRANDON (English) Sword; hill afire. Variations: *Bran, Brandan, Branden, Brandin, Brandyn.*

BRANT (English) Proud. Variation: *Brannt.*

BRAXTON (English) Literally, Brock's town.

BRENDAN (Irish) Little raven. Brendan was also an Irish saint nicknamed the Voyager who, rumor has it, was the first Irishman to sail to America. Variations: *Brenden, Brendin, Brendon.*

BRENT (English) Mountaintop. Though Brent is very popular today, it has been used as a first name only for the last 50 years or so. Variations: *Breneon, Brentan, Brentin, Brenton, Brentyn.*

BRETT (English) British man. Brett is a name that is more popular in Australia than it is on these shores. Brett is also frequently used as a girls' name today. Variations: *Bret, Brette, Bretton, Brit, Britt.*

BRIAN (Celtic) Brave; virtuous. Variations: *Briano, Brien, Brion, Bryan, Bryon.*

BRIGHTON (English) Town in Britain.

BRODERICK (Scottish) Brother. Variations: *Brod, Broddy, Broderic, Brodric, Brodrick.*

BRONSON (English) Dark man's son. Variations: *Bron, Bronnson, Bronsen, Bronsin, Bronsonn, Bronsson.*

BROOK (English) Brook; stream. Variations: *Brooke, Brookes, Brooks.*

BRUCE (English) Thick brush. Variations: *Brucey, Brucie.*

BRYSON (English) Nobleman's son.

BYRON (English) Cow barn. Variation: *Biron.*

CALDWELL (English) Stream; cold well. Variation: *Cal*.

CALEB (Hebrew) Brave; dog. Caleb was a popular name among Puritans in the United States, since the Biblical Caleb was one of the people who spent time wandering with Moses on his excursion in the wilderness. Variations: *Cale, Kalb, Kaleb*.

CALEY (Irish) Slender.

CALVIN (English) Bald. Variations: *Cal, Calvino, Kalvin*.

CAMERON (Gaelic) Crooked nose or river. Variation: *Camron*.

CAREY (Welsh) Near a castle. Variation: *Cary*.

CARL (English) Man. Variation: *Karl*.

CARLOS (Spanish) Man. Spanish version of Charles. Variations: *Carlino, Carlo, Carolo*.

CARSON (English) Son of a family from a marsh. Variation: *Karsen*.

CASEY (Irish) Observant. Popular among both girls and boys. Variations: *Cacey, Cayce, Caycey, Kasey*.

CASSIDY (Irish) Smart. It literally translates from O'Caiside, which means one who dwells in an area of Ireland called Caiside. Caiside itself means bent love, which somehow turned into "smart." Variation: *Cassady*.

CHAD (English) Protector. Strong, one-syllable names became popular for a while in the late twentieth century. Variations: *Chadd, Chadwick*.

CHANCE (English) Good fortune.

CHANDLER (English) Candle maker. This name has become popular in the last few years.

CHAPMAN (English) Peddler. Variations: *Chap, Chappy*.

CHARLES (English) Man. Charles has spawned a number of variations in all cultures throughout the centuries. The name has a rich and varied history, as the name of the patron saint of Catholic bishops, cartoon characters, and a slew of great actors. Variations: *Charley, Charlie, Chas, Chaz, Chick, Chip, Chuck.*

CHARLTON (English) House where Charles lives. Variations: *Carleton, Carlton.*

CHASE (English) Hunter. Variations: *Chace, Chaise.*

CHASIN (Hebrew) Strong. Variations: *Chason, Hasin, Hassin.*

CHEN (Chinese) Great.

CHESTER (English) Campsite. Variations: *Cheston, Chet.*

CHIP (English) Nickname for Charles that is sometimes given as the full name.

CHRISTOPHER (English) One who holds Christ in his heart. Famous Christophers include St. Christopher, the patron saint of people who travel, Winnie-the-Pooh's friend Christopher Robin, and explorer Christopher Columbus. Variations: *Chris, Christof, Christofer, Christoff, Christoffer, Christoforus, Christoph, Christophe, Christophoros, Christos, Christos, Cris, Cristobal, Cristoforo, Kit, Kitt, Kristofer, Kristofor.*

CLARENCE (English) Clear. Variations: *Clair, Clarance, Clare, Clarey.*

CLARK (English) Scholar. Variations: *Clarke, Clerc, Clerk.*

CLAY (English) Maker of clay.

CLIFFORD (English) Place to cross a river near a cliff. Variations: *Cliff, Clyff, Clyfford.*

CODY (English) Cushion. Cody used to be known as a town in Wyoming and the name of various Western outlaws from the second part of the nineteenth century.

Cody is not only popular for boys but also for girls. Variations: *Codey, Codie, Coty, Kodey, Kodie, Kody.*

COLBY (English) Dark farm. Variation: *Collby.*

COLIN (English) Triumphant people; also, young boy. Colin and its various spellings have become popular for boys, and to a lesser extent, girls, in the last 10 years or so. Variations: *Colan, Cole, Collin, Colyn.*

COLWYN (Welsh) River in Wales. Variations: *Colwin, Colwynn.*

CONNOR (Irish) Much desire. Another popular name that is starting to appear in both sexes more frequently. Variations: *Conner, Conor.*

COREY (Irish) The hollow. Variations: *Corin, Correy, Cory, Korey.*

COSMO (Greek) Order. Cosmo is the Patron Saint of Milan and of doctors. Variations: *Cos, Cosimo, Cosme.*

CRAIG (Welsh) Rock. Variation: *Kraig.*

DAKOTA (Dakota) Friend. Dakota is also used as a name for girls, as are many of the other currently popular names that describe locations.

DALE (English) One who lives in a dale or valley. Variations: *Dal, Daley, Daly, Dayle.*

DALLAS (Scottish) Town in Scotland and a city in Texas. Dallas can also be used as a name for girls.

DALTON (English) A town in a valley. Variations: Dallton, Dalten.

DAMIAN (Greek) Tame. Damian was a popular name in the '70s, until its appearance in several horror movies. Variations: *Dameon, Damiano, Damien, Damion, Damyan, Damyen, Damyon.*

DANIEL (Hebrew) God is my judge. Variations: *Dan, Danakas, Danek, Dani, Daniele, Daniels, Danil, Danila, Danilkar, Danilo, Danko, Dannie, Danniel, Danny, Dano, Danya, Danylets, Danylo, Dasco, Donois, Dusan.*

DANTE (Latin) Everlasting. Variations: *Dontae, Donte*.

DARIN (Greek) Gift. Variations: *Dare, Daron, Darren, Darrin, Darron*.

DARNELL (English) Hidden area. Variations: *Darnal, Darnall, Darnel*.

DARREN (Gaelic) Great. Variations: *Daran, Daren, ~~Derek~~ Darin, Darran, Darrin, Darron, Darryn, Daryn*.

DARRYL (English) An English last name. Darryl was a popular name in the '80s. Variations: *Darrel, Darrell, Darrill, Darrol, Darryll, Daryl, Daryll*.

DAVID (Hebrew) Cherished. The name has significance in both the Christian and Jewish religions: David is one of the patron saints of Wales, while the Star of David is the cornerstone symbol of Judaism. Variations: *Dave, Daveed, Davi, Davidek, Davie, Davy, Dewey, Dodya*.

DAVIS (English) Son of David. Variations: *Davison, Dawson*.

DEAN (English) Valley. Variations: *Deane, Dene*.

DELANEY (Irish) Child of a competitor. Variations: *Delaine, Delainey, Delainy, Delane, Delany.*

DELBERT (English) Sunny day.

DELMAR (Spanish) Oceanside. Variations: *Delmer, Delmor, Delmore.*

DEMARCO (African-American) Demarco is a newly created name that literally means of Mark. Variations: *D'Marcus, Damarcus, Demarcus, Demario, Demarkis, Demarkus.*

DEMETRIUS (Greek) Lover of the earth. Variations: *Demeter, Demetre, Demetri, Demetrio, Demetris, Demetrois, Dimetre, Dimitri, Dimitry, Dmitri, Dmitrios, Dmitry.*

DENNIS (Greek) One who follows Dionysius, the Greek god of wine. Denis is also the patron saint of France. Variations: *Denies, Denis, Denka, Dennes, Denney, Denny, Dennys, Denys.*

DENZELL (African-American) Unknown definition. Variations: *Denzel, Denziel, Denzil, Denzill, Denzyl.*

DEREK (English) Leader. Variations: *Dereck, Derick, Derik, Derreck, Derrek, Derrick, Derrik, Deryck, Deryk.*

DERMOT (Irish) Free of jealousy. Variations: *Dermod, Dermott.*

DESHAWN (African-American) Newly created. Variations: *D'chaun, DaShaun, Dashawn, DeSean, DeShaun, Deshaun.*

DESMOND (Irish) From South Munster, an old civilization in Ireland. Variations: *Desmund, Dezmond.*

DEWAYNE (African-American) Newly created. Variations: *D'Wayne, DeWayne.*

DEXTER (Latin) Right-handed. Variation: *Dex.*

DILLON (Irish) Loyal. Variations: *Dillan, Dilon, Dilyn.*

DION (African-American) God. Variations: *Deion, DeOn, Deon.*

DOMINICK (English) Lord. Variations: *Dom, Dome, Domek, Domenic, Domenico, Domicio, Domingo, Domingos, Dominic,*

Dominik, Dominique, Domo, Domokos, Nic, Nick, Nik.

DONOVAN (Irish) Dark. Variations: *Don, Donavan, Donavon, Donoven, Donovon.*

DOUGLAS (English) Dark water. River in Ireland. Common Scottish last name. Variations: *Doug, Douglass.*

DREW (English) Wise. Diminutive of Andrew. Variations: *Drewe, Dru.*

DYLAN (Welsh) Son of the ocean. Variations: *Dillan, Dillon.*

EARL (English) Leader; nobleman. Variations: *Earle, Earlie, Early, Erl, Erle, Errol, Erryl.*

EATON (English) Town on a river. Variations: *Eatton, Eton, Eyton.*

EDEN (Hebrew) Delight. Variations: *Eaden, Eadin, Edan, Edin.*

EDGAR (English) Wealthy man who holds a spear. Variations: *Edgard, Edgardo.*

EDISON (English) Edward's son. Variations: *Ed, Eddison, Edson.*

EDWARD (English) Guardian of property. Variations: *Ed, Eddie, Edouard, Eduardo, Edvard.*

EDWIN (English) Rich friend. Variation: *Edwyn.*

ELAN (Hebrew) Tree. Variation: *Ilan.*

ELDRIDGE (German) Wise leader.

ELI (Hebrew) God is great. Variations: *Elie, Ely.*

ELIJAH (Hebrew) The Lord is my God. Variations: *Elek, Elias, Eliasz, Elie, Eliya, Eliyahu, Ellis, Elya.*

ELLERY (English) Island with elder trees. Last name. Variation: *Ellary.*

ELLIOT (English) God on high. Variations: *Eliot, Eliott, Elliott.*

ELMORE (English) Valley with elm trees.

EMANUEL (Hebrew) God is among us. The name given to the Messiah. Variations: *Emmanuel, Emmanuil; Immanuel, Manny, Manuel.*

EMERY (German) Leader of the house. Variations: *Emmery, Emory.*

ENNIS (Gaelic) Only choice.

ENZO (Italian) To win.

ERIC (Scandinavian) Ruler of the people. Variations: *Erek, Erich, Erick, Erico, Erik.*

ERROL (Scottish) Area in Scotland. Variations: *Erroll, Erryl.*

ERWIN (English) A boar and a friend. Variations: *Erwinek, Erwyn, Erwynn, Irwin.*

ETHAN (Hebrew) Steady. Variations: *Eitan, Etan.*

ETIENNE (French) Crown. Variation of Stephen.

EVAN (Welsh) God is good. Evan is a version of John that is picking up speed as a common name for American boys today. Variations: *Ev, Evann, Evans, Evin, Ewan.*

EVANDER (Scottish) Good man.

EVERETT (English) Powerful as a boar. Everett is most commonly known as a last name. Variations: *Everard, Everet, Everhard, Everitt.*

EZEKIEL (Hebrew) The strength of God. Variation: *Zeke.*

EZIO (Italian) Unknown definition.

FABIAN (Latin) One who grows beans. Variations: *Faba, Fabek, Faber, Fabert, Fabiano, Fabien, Fabio, Fabius, Fabiyan, Fabyan, Fabyen.*

FABRON (French) Blacksmith. Variations: *Fabre, Fabroni.*

FAGAN (Irish) Eager child. Variation: *Fagin.*

FAHIM (Hindu) Intelligent.

FAIRLEIGH (English) Meadow with bulls. Variations: *Fairlay, Fairlee, Fairlie, Farleigh, Farley.*

FALKNER (English) Falcon trainer. Variations: *Falconer, Falconner, Faulkner, Fowler.*

FARAJ (Arabic) Cure. Variation: *Farag.*

FARIS (Arabic) Knight.

FARON (English) Unknown definition. Last name. Variations: *Faran, Farin, Farran, Farrin, Farron, Farrun, Farun.*

FARRELL (Irish) Courageous man. Variations: *Farall, Farrel, Farrill, Farryll, Ferrel, Ferrell, Ferrill, Ferryl.*

FARROW (Irish) Unknown definition. Last name.

FENTON (English) Town by a swamp.

FERDINAND (German) Brave traveler. Ferdinand is a very old name. It was used by Shakespeare in *Love's Labour's Lost* as well as *The Tempest*. Variations: *Ferdinando, Ferdynand, Fernand, Fernando.*

FIELDING (English) In the field. Variation: *Field.*

FINIAN (Irish) Fair. The musical *Finian's Rainbow* is how most people were first exposed to this name. Variations: *Finnian, Fionan, Fionn.*

FITCH (English) Name of a mammal similar to a ferret.

FITZPATRICK (Irish) Son of a statesman.

FLANNERY (Irish) Red hair. Variations: *Flaine, Flann, Flannan.*

FLETCHER (English) One who makes arrows. Variation: *Fletch.*

FLOYD (Welsh) Gray hair.

FLYNN (Irish) Red-haired man's son. Variations: *Flin, Flinn, Flyn.*

FOREST (French) Woods. Variations: *Forester, Forrest, Forrester, Forster, Foster.*

FRANCIS (Latin) Frenchman. Francis was frequently in the top 10 list of names from the late nineteenth century through the '40s. Variations: *Fran, Franc, Franchot, Francisco, Franco, Francois, Frank, Frankie, Franky.*

FRANKLIN (English) A free property owner. Variations: *Frank, Franki, Frankie, Franklyn, Franklynn, Franky.*

FRANZ (German) Frenchman. Variations: *Frans, Franzen, Franzl.*

FRASER (English) Town in France. Variations: *Frasier, Fraze, Frazer, Frazier.*

FREDERICK (German) Merciful leader. Variations: *Fred, Freddie, Freddy, Fredek, Frederich, Frederico, Frederik, Fredric, Fredrick, Friedrich, Fritz.*

FRITZ (German) Peaceful ruler. Fritz started out as a nickname for Frederick, but started to appear as an independent name among babies born in the late nineteenth century. Variations: *Fritzchen, Fritzroy.*

FULLER (English) One who shrinks cloth.

GABRIEL (Hebrew) Man of God. Variations: *Gab, Gabby, Gabe, Gabi, Gabko, Gabo, Gabor, Gabriele, Gabrielli, Gabriello, Gabris, Gabys, Gavi, Gavriel.*

GALEN (Greek) Healer. Variation: *Galeno*.

GALLAGHER (Irish) Foreign partner.

GALVIN (Irish) Sparrow. Variations: *Gallven, Gallvin, Galvan, Galven*.

GARETH (Welsh) Gentle. Variations: *Garith, Garreth, Garyth*.

GARRICK (English) He who rules with a spear. Variations: *Garreck, Garryck, Garyk*.

GARTH (English) Gardener.

GARY (English) Spear. Variations: *Garey, Garrey, Garry*.

GAVIN (Welsh) White falcon. Variations: *Gavan, Gaven, Gavyn, Gawain, Gawaine, Gawayn, Gawayne, Gawen*.

GAYNOR (Irish) Son of a pale man.

GEARY (English) Changeable. Variation: *Gearey*.

GENE (English) Well born. Derived from Eugene. Variations: *Genek, Genio, Genka, Genya*.

GEOFFREY (German) Peace. Alternative spelling for Jeffrey.

GEORGE (Greek) Farmer. George seems to be making a mini-comeback, particularly among parents who wish to honor an older relative with the name. Variations: *Georg, Georges, Georgi, Georgios, Georgy, Giorgio, Giorgos.*

GERALD (German) Ruler with a spear. Variations: *Geralde, Geraldo, Geraud, Gerrald, Gerrold, Gerry, Jerald, Jeralde, Jeraud, Jerold, Jerrald, Jerrold, Jerry.*

GERARD (German) Brave with a spear. Variations: *Garrard, Gerhard, Gerrard, Gerrit, Gerry.*

GERONIMO (Native American: Apache) A famous Apache Indian chief.

GERSHOM (Hebrew) Exile. Variations: *Gersham, Gershon, Gerson.*

GIANCARLO (Italian) Combination of John and Charles.

GILBERT (German) Bright pledge. Variations: *Gib, Gil, Gilberto.*

GILES (English) Shield bearer. Variations: *Gil, Gilles, Gyles.*

GILMORE (Irish) Servant of the Virgin Mary.
Variations: *Gillmore, Gillmour, Gilmour, Giolle Maire.*

GLEN (Irish) Narrow valley. Variation: *Glenn.*

GORDON (English) Round hill. Variations: *Gordan, Gorden, Gordie, Gordy.*

GRAHAM (English) Gray house. Variations: *Graeham, Graeme, Grahame, Gram.*

GRANT (Scottish) Great.

GRAYSON (English) Son of a man with gray hair. Variation: *Greyson.*

GREGORY (Greek) Observant. Gregory and its off-shoots have been popular in this country since Gregory Peck appeared in *To Kill a Mockingbird.* Before that watershed event, it was more frequently chosen by popes—16 of them, to be precise. Variations: *Greg, Gregg, Gregoire, Gregor, Gregorio, Gregorios, Gregos, Greig, Gries, Grigor.*

GRIFFIN (Latin) One with a hooked nose. Variations: *Griff, Griffon, Gryphon.*

GUNNAR (Scandinavian) Battle. Variations: *Gun, Gunder.*

GUS (English) Majestic. Gus was originally a shortened form of Augustus, but came into its own as an independent name over the course of the last century.

HABIB (Arabic) Dear.

HAKEEM (Arabic) Wise. Hakeem is common in Muslim countries, as it is one of the 99 qualities of Allah that are detailed in the Koran, but it is becoming more popular here, particularly among African-American and Muslim families. Variations: *Hakem, Hakim.*

HALSEY (English) The island that belongs to Hal. Variations: *Hallsey, Hallsy, Halsy.*

HAMID (Arabic) Greatly praised. Derivative of Mohammed. Variations: *Hammad, Hammed.*

HAMILTON (English) Fortified castle. Variation: *Hamelton.*

HAMISH (Scottish) He who removes. Hamish, which is appearing more frequently also has its roots in Yiddish, where it means comfortable.

HANK (English) Ruler of the estate. Diminutive of Henry. Hank is a down-home, unpretentious name, partly because of the famous men who have lived with the name—Hank Aaron and Hank Williams

HARLAN (English) Army land. Variations: *Harland, Harlen, Harlenn, Harlin, Harlyn, Harlynn.*

HAROLD (English) Army ruler. Variations: *Hal, Harailt, Harald, Haraldo, Haralds, Haroldas, Haroldo.*

HARPER (English) Harp player. Harper is also used as a girls' name.

HARRISON (English) Harry's son. Variation: *Harrisen.*

HARRY (English) Ruler at home. Variation of Henry. Variations: *Harrey, Harri, Harrie.*

HARTWELL (English) Well where stags drink. Variations: *Harwell, Harwill.*

HARVEY (French) Eager for battle. Harvey is back with a vengeance, and growing in popularity. Variations: *Herve, Hervey*.

HASIM (Arabic) To determine.

HAYDEN (English) Hill of heather; (Welsh) Valley with hedges. Though Hayden and its variants are quite popular across the ocean in Great Britain and Wales, the name is just beginning to catch on in this country. Variations: *Aidan, Haddan, Haddon, Haden, Hadon, Hadyn, Haydn, Haydon*.

HAYWARD (English) Protector of hedged area.

HEINRICH (German) Ruler of the estate. Variation of Henry. Variations: *Heinrick, Heinrik, Henrik, Henrique, Henryk*.

HELMUT (French) Helmet.

HENRY (German) Ruler of the house. Like Harry, another previously unpopular name in recent decades, Henry is one of the more popular choices around. Variations: *Henery, Henri, Henrik, Henrique, Henryk*.

HERBERT (German) Shining army. Variations: *Heibert, Herb, Herbie.*

HERMAN (German) Army man. Herman Melville, the author of *Moby Dick,* is among the most famous recipients of the name. Variations: *Hermann, Hermon.*

HILLEL (Hebrew) Highly praised. Jewish families are choosing this name more frequently for their sons. Hillel was the name of one of the first great Talmudic scholars.

HIRSH (Hebrew) Deer. Variations: *Hersch, Herschel, Hersh, Hershel, Hersz, Hertz, Hertzel, Herz, Herzl, Heschel, Hesh, Hirsch, Hirschel.*

HOLBROOK (English) Brook near the hollow. Variation: *Holbrooke.*

HOLDEN (English) Hollow valley.

HORACE (Latin) Old Roman clan name. Variations: *Horacio, Horatio.*

HOSEA (Hebrew) Deliverance. Variations: *Hoseia, Hosheia.*

HOWARD (English) Observer. Last name. Variation: *Howie.*

HOWELL (Welsh) Exceptional.

HOYT (Irish) Spirit.

IAN (Scottish) God is good. Ian hit its peak in both Britain and the United States in the mid-'60s. Variations: *Ean, Iain, Iancu, Ianos.*

IBRAHIM (Arabic) Father of many. Variation of Abraham.

ICARUS (Greek) Greek mythological figure who flew too close to the sun; his wings, attached to his body with wax, fell off and he plummeted to earth.

IMRAN (Arabic) Host.

INCENCIO (Spanish) White one.

INGHAM (English) Area in Britain.

INNES (Scottish) Island. Variations: *Inness, Innis, Inniss.*

IRA (Hebrew) Observant.

IRVIN (Scottish) Beautiful. Variation: *Irvine.*

IRVING (English) Sea friend. Variation: *Irv.*

ISAAC (Hebrew) Laughter. Variations: *Isaak, Isak, Itzak, Ixaka, Izaak.*

ISAIAH (Hebrew) God helps me. Variations: *Isa, Isaia, Isia, Isiah, Issiah.*

ISHA (Hindu) Lord.

ISHMAEL (Hebrew) God will hear. Variations: *Ismael, Ismail, Yishmael.*

ISRAEL (Hebrew) Struggle with God. Variation: *Yisrael.*

IVAN (Czech) God is good. Variations: *Ivanchik, Ivanek, Ivano, Ivas.*

IVES (English) Yew wood; archer. Variations: *Ivo, Ivon, Yves.*

IVORY (African-American) Ivory.

JABBAR (Hindu) One who comforts.

JACKSON (English) Son of Jack. Variation: *Jakson*.

JACOB (Hebrew) Supplanter or heel. Jacob first appears in the book of Genesis in the Bible; Jacob was the youngest son of Isaac and Rebecca. It is very popular among parents these days, possibly because it displays a sense of forthrightness and openness. Variations: *Jaco, Jacobus, Jacoby, Jacquet, Jakab, Jake, Jakie, Jakiv, Jakob, Jakov, Jakub, Jakubek, Kiva, Kivi*.

JAGGER (English) To haul something.

JAKEEM (Arabic) Noble.

JAMAL (Arabic) Handsome. Variations: *Gamal, Gamil, Jamaal, Jamahl, Jamall, Jameel, Jamel, Jamell, Jamil, Jamill, Jammal*.

JAMES (English) He who replaces. Variation of Jacob. James—by itself and in its many incarnations—has never really gone out of style. Variations:

Jacques, Jaime, Jaimey, Jaimie, Jaimito, Jamey, Jamie, Jayme, Jaymes, Jaymie, Jim, Jimi, Jimmey, Jimmie, Jimmy.

JAMESON (English) Son of James. Variations: *Jamieson, Jamison.*

JARED (Hebrew) Descend. Jared, with its many variants, has been very popular since the mid-'60s, when it first began to appear with some regularity. Variations: *Jarad, Jarid, Jarod, Jarrad, Jarred, Jerad, Jered, Jerod, Jerrad, Jerrod, Jerryd, Yarden, Yared.*

JARETH (African-American) Newly created. Variations: *Jarreth, Jerth.*

JARON (Hebrew) To shout. Variations: *Gerron, Jaran, Jaren, Jarin, Jarran, Jarren, Jarron, Jeran, Jeren, Jeron, Jerrin, Jerron.*

JARRETT (English) Brave with a spear. Variations: *Jarret, Jarrete.*

JARVIS (German). Honorable. Variation: *Jervis.*

JASON (Hebrew) God is my salvation. Variations: *Jace, Jacen, Jaison, Jase, Jasen, Jayce, Jaycen, Jaysen, Jayson.*

JASPER (English) Wealthy one. Variation: *Jaspar.*

JAY (Latin) Blue jay. Variations: *Jae, Jai, Jave, Jaye, Jeays, Jeyes.*

JEDIDIAH (Hebrew) Beloved of God. Variations: *Jed, Jedd, Jedediah, Jedidia, Yedidia, Yedidiah, Yedidya.*

JEFFREY (German) Peace. Jeffrey was one of the most popular names in the United States in the '70s. When parents choose it today, they tend to select one of its more unusual spellings. Variations: *Geoff, Geoffrey, Geoffry, Gioffredo, Jeff, Jefferies, Jeffery, Jeffries, Jeffry, Jefry.*

JEREMY (Hebrew) The Lord exalts. Jeremy has been a popular name among American parents in the last couple of decades. Variations: *Jem, Jemmie, Jemmy, Jeramee, Jeramey, Jeramie, Jere, Jereme, Jeremey, Jeremi, Jeremia, Jeremias, Jeremie, Jerimiah, Jeromy, Jerr, Jerrie, Jerry.*

JERMAINE (German) German. Variations: *Jermain, Jermane, Jermayne.*

JEROME (Greek) Sacred name. Name of a saint. Variations: *Jeron, Jerone, Jerrome.*

JERRELL (African-American) Newly created. Variations: *Gerrell, Jarell, Jarrel, Jarrell, Jeriel, Jerriel, Jerul.*

JESSE (Hebrew) God exists. Variations: *Jesiah, Jess, Jessey, Jessie, Jessy.*

JETT (English) Airplane.

JOACHIM (Hebrew) God will determine. Variations: *Joaquim, Joaquin.*

JOEL (Hebrew) God is Lord.

JOERGEN (Scandinavian) Farmer.

JOHN (Hebrew) God is good. If you count all of the variations, spellings, and the language usages around the world, it's possible that more boys are named John than any other name. With this prestige and a wide variety of Johns to choose from, it's a good bet that John in one or more of its forms will never be out of style. Variations: *Jack, Jackie, Jacky, Joao, Jock, Jockel, Jocko, Johan, Johann, Johannes, Johnie, Johnnie, Johnny, Jon, Jonam, Jone, Jonelis, Jonnie, Jonny, Jonukas, Jonutis, Jovan, Jovanus, Jovi, Jovin, Jovito, Jovon, Juan, Juanito.*

JONAH (Hebrew) Dove. Biblical book. Variations: *Jonas, Yonah, Yonas, Yunus.*

JONATHAN (Hebrew) Gift from God. In the Bible, Jonathan was King Saul's oldest son and was best known as King David's best friend. Parents have liked Jonathan because it is based on a classic name—John—but is more distinctive. Variations: *Johnathan, Johnathen, Johnathon, Jon, Jonathen, Jonathon, Jonnie, Jonny, Jonothon.*

JORDAN (Hebrew) To descend. Jordan is a unisex name as well as an occasional last name, which has helped to make it as popular as it is. During the Crusades, the name caught on when soldiers brought water from the River Jordan back home with them to baptize their children. Variations: *Jorden, Jordy, Jori, Jorrin.*

JOSEPH (Hebrew) God will increase. Joseph is perhaps best known as Mary's husband. This fact, and its many varieties in America and around the world, may be the reason why the name has never fallen out of style. Variations: *Jodi, Jodie, Jody, Jose, Josecito, Josef, Joselito, Josephe, Josephus, Josip.*

JOSHUA (Hebrew) God is my salvation. Joshua was the leader of the Jews after Moses, and a book in the Bible is named for him. However, Joshua has only started to become popular since the '60s, although other Biblical names have been used for centuries. Variations: *Josh, Joshuah.*

JOSIAH (Hebrew) God supports. Variations: *Josia, Josias, Josua.*

JUDE (Hebrew) Praise God. Variations: *Juda, Judah, Judas, Judd, Judson.*

JULIAN (Latin) Version of Julius. Saint. Variations: *Julien, Julion, Julyan.*

JUNIOR (English) Young.

KADEEM (African-American) Newly created.

KAHIL (Turkish) Young. Kahil is a name that is popular in many different countries, not just Turkey. In Hebrew, it means perfect; in Greece, it means beautiful. Up until the '70s the form of the name we had most often seen was Cahil, the English version of this name. However, African-American families have made this name more popular in the United States. Variations: *Cahil, Kahlil, Kaleel, Khaleel, Khalil.*

KAI (Hawaiian) Sea.

KAMAL (Arabic) Perfect. Like many of the other Arabic and Turkish names for boys that begin with "K," Kamal is becoming more popular in this country, especially among African-American families. Variations: *Kameel, Kamil.*

KANE (Welsh) Beautiful; (Japanese) Golden. In America, Kane is becoming more popular for both boys and girls. Variations: *Kain, Kaine, Kayne, Keanu.*

KAREEM (Arabic) Generous. Its definition, generous, is one of the 99 qualities ascribed to God in the Koran. Variations: *Karim, Karime.*

KARL (German) Man. Variations: *Karlen, Karlens, Karlin.*

KASPAR (Persian) Protector of wealth. Variation: *Kasper.*

KEATON (English) Hawk nest. Variations: *Keeton, Keiton, Keyton.*

KEEGAN (Irish) Small and passionate. Variations: *Kagen, Keagan, Keegen, Kegan.*

KEELEY (Irish) Handsome. Variations: *Kealey, Kealy, Keelie, Keely.*

KEITH (Scottish) Forest.

KELLY (Irish) Warrior. Not too long ago, Kelly was a name given in equal measure to both boys and

girls. But today, a boy with the name of Kelly is a rare thing indeed. Variations: *Kelley, Kellie.*

KELSEY (English) Island. Variations: *Kelsie, Kelsy.*

KENDALL (English) Last name. Valley of the river Kent. Variations: *Kendal, Kendell.*

KENNEDY (Irish) Helmeted ruler. In the '60s, Kennedy was a name given to boys to honor the esteemed political family from Massachusetts. Variations: *Canaday, Canady, Kenneday.*

KENNETH (Irish) Handsome; sprung from fire. Variations: *Ken, Kendall, Kenney, Kennie, Kennith, Kenny, Kenyon.*

KENT (English) County in England.

KERRY (Irish) County in Ireland. Variations: *Kerrey, Kerrie.*

KERWIN (Irish) Dark. Variations: *Kerwen, Kerwinn, Kerwyn, Kirwin.*

KESHON (African-American) Version of Sean. Variations: *Ke Sean, Ke Shon, Kesean.*

KEVIN (Irish) Handsome. Today, Kevin, traditionally a name given to Irish Catholic boys, is used in a more multidenominational fashion than before. Variations: *Kavan, Kev, Kevan, Keven, Kevon, Kevyn.*

KIRBY (English) Village of the church. Variations: *Kerbey, Kerbi, Kerbie, Kirbey, Kirbie.*

KIRK (Scandinavian: Norwegian) Church. Variations: *Kerk, Kirke.*

KITO (African: Swahili) Jewel.

KLAUS (German) Victorious people. Short for Nicholas. Variations: *Claes, Claus, Clause, Klaas, Klaes.*

KNOWLES (English) Grassy hill. Variations: *Knolls, Nowles.*

KNOX (English) Hills.

KNUTE (Scandinavian: Danish) Knot.

KOJO (African: Ghanian) Born on Monday.

KWAN (Korean) Powerful.

KYLE (Scottish) Narrow land. Though Kyle is also a popular choice for girls these days, the name for boys made it into the top 20 most popular names of the '90s. In Hebrew, it means crowned with laurel. Variations: *Kiel, Kile, Ky, Kyele, Kyler.*

KYROS (Greek) Master.

LA VONN (African-American) The small one. Variations: *La Vaun, La Voun.*

LAMBERT (German) Bright land. Variations: *Lambard, Lampard;* (Scandinavian) Famous land. Variation: *Lammert.*

LANGSTON (English) Long town. Variations: *Langsden, Langsdon.*

LASZLO (Hungarian) Famous leader. Variations: *Laslo, Lazuli.*

LAWRENCE (English) Crowned with laurel. Variations: *Larry, Laurance, Laurence, Laurencio, Laurens, Laurent, Laurenz, Laurie, Lauris, Laurus,*

Lawrance, Lawrey, Lawrie, Lawry, Loren, Lorence, Lorencz, Lorens, Lorenzo, Lorin, Lorry, Lowrance.

LAWSON (English) Son of Lawrence.

LAWTON (English) Town on a hill. Variation: *Laughton.*

LEE (English) Meadow. The name Lee has always been hugely popular, both as a first and last name and as a good name for both boys and girls. Variation: *Leigh.*

LEIF (Scandinavian: Norwegian) Beloved. Variations: *Leaf, Lief.*

LEIGHTON (English) Town by the meadow. Variations: *Layton, Leyton.*

LENNOX (Scottish) Many elm trees. Variation: *Lenox.*

LEON (Greek) Lion. Variations: *Leo, Leonas, Leone, Leonek, Leonidas, Leosko.*

LEONARD (German) Bold as a lion. Given the name's positive and somewhat exotic connotations,

Leonard might be making a comeback. Variations: *Len, Lenard, Lennard, Lenny, Leonardo, Leonek, Leonhard, Leonhards, Leonid, Leontes, Lienard, Linek, Lon, Lonnie, Lonny.*

LEROY (French) The king. Variations: *Le Roy, LeeRoy, Leeroy, LeRoi, Leroi, LeRoy.*

LESLIE (Scottish) Low meadow. Variations: *Les, Leslea, Lesley, Lesly, Lezly.*

LESTER (English) Last name. Area in Britain, Leicester. Like its cousin Leslie, Lester has gone out of fashion. Variation: *Les.*

LEVI (Hebrew) Attached. Variations: *Levey, Levin, Levon, Levy.*

LEYLAND (English) Uncultivated land.

LINCOLN (English) Variations: *Linc, Link.*

LINDELL (English) Valley of the linden trees. Variations: *Lindall, Lindel, Lyndall, Lyndell.*

LINDSAY (English) Island of linden trees. Variations: *Lindsee, Lindsey, Lindsy, Linsay, Linsey, Lyndsay, Lyndsey.*

LIONEL (Latin) Little lion. Variations: *Leonel, Lionell, Lionello, Lonell, Lonnell.*

LIVINGSTON (English) Leif's settlement. Variation: *Livingstone.*

LLOYD (Welsh) Gray or sacred. Variation: *Loyd.*

LOGAN (Irish) Hollow in a meadow.

LORNE (Scottish) Area in Scotland. Variation: *Lorn.*

LOUDON (German) A low valley. Variations: *Louden, Lowden, Lowdon.*

LOUIS (French) Famous warrior. Louis is an old and highly esteemed French name. Dating from the sixth century A.D., Louis has been the name of no fewer than 18 kings in France. Variations: *Lew, Lewe, Lotario, Lothair, Lothar, Lothario, Lou, Luigi, Luis.*

LOWELL (English) Young wolf. Variation: *Lowel.*

LUCAS (English) An area in southern Italy. Variations: *Loukas, Luc, Lukas, Luke.*

LUCIUS (Latin) Light. Variations: *Luca, Lucan, Lucca, Luce, Lucian, Luciano, Lucias, Lucien, Lucio.*

LUDWIG (German) Famous soldier.

LUTHER (German) Army people. Luther has been popular in the past as a middle name, probably owing to Martin Luther King, Jr.

LYLE (French) The island. Variations: *Lisle, Ly, Lyall, Lyell, Lysle.*

LYNDEN (English) Hill with lime trees. Variations: *Linden, Lyndon, Lynne.*

LYSANDER (Greek) Liberator. Variation: *Lisandro.*

MAC (Scottish) Son of. Variation: *Mack.*

MACAULAY (Scottish) Son of the moral one.

MACBRIDE (Irish) Son of Saint Brigid. Variations: *Macbryde, McBride.*

MACDONALD (Scottish) Son of Donald. The Macdonalds were a powerful Scottish clan. Variations: *MacDonald, McDonald.*

MACGOWAN (Irish) Son of the blacksmith. Variations: *MacGowan, Magowan, McGowan.*

MACKENZIE (Irish) Son of a wise leader. Variations: *Mack, MacKenzie, Mackey, Mackie, McKenzie.*

MACKINLEY (Irish) Learned ruler. Variations: *MacKinley, McKinley.*

MADDOX (Welsh) Generous. Variations: *Maddock, Madock, Madox.*

MADISON (English) Son of the mighty warrior. Whether it's an avenue, a president, or a baby name, Madison is an up-and-comer, for both girls and boys. Variations: *Maddie, Maddison, Maddy, Madisson.*

MADU (African: Nigerian) People.

MAGUIRE (Irish) Son of the beige man. Variations: *MacGuire, McGuire, McGwire.*

MAKOTO (Japanese) Honesty.

MALCOLM (English) A servant. Malcolm's burgeoning popularity has probably been helped along by Malcolm X. Variations: *Malcolum, Malcom, Malkolm.*

MALLORY (French) Sad. Variations: *Mallery, Mallorie, Malory.*

MANDELA (African-American) Name of the South African president.

MANFRED (English) Man of peace. Variations: *Manafred, Manafryd, Manfrid, Manfried, Mannfred, Mannfryd.*

MANLEY (English) Man's meadow. Variations: *Manlea, Manleigh, Manly.*

MANSFIELD (English) Field by a river.

MANSUR (Arabic) Divine assistance. Variation: *Mansour.*

MARCUS (Latin) Warlike. Variations: *Marco, Marcos.*

MARIO (Italian) Roman clan name.

MARK (English) Warlike. Variations: *Marc, Marco, Marko, Markos.*

MARSHALL (French) One who cares for horses. Because this name conveys such an in-charge tone, perhaps people in the military will prefer it for their kids, but for the rest of us, expect it to be quite an unusual choice. Variations: *Marschal, Marsh, Marshal.*

MARTIN (Latin) Warlike. Martin was always much more popular as a last name than a first name, except of course in the case of the Reverend Martin Luther King, Jr., who was first christened with the name Michael. Variations: *Mart, Martan, Martel, Marten, Martey, Martie, Martinas, Martiniano, Martinka, Martino, Martinos, Martins, Marto, Marton, Marty, Martyn, Mertin.*

MARVIN (English) Mariner. Variations: *Marv, Marvyn.*

MASON (French) Stone carver or worker. Variations: *Mace, Masson.*

MATTHEW (Hebrew) Gift of the Lord. Matthew has been a very popular name, both 2,000 years ago and today. Variations: *Mateo, Mateus, Mathe, Mathew, Mathia, Mathias, Mathieu, Matias, Matt, Matteo, Matthaus, Matthia, Matthias, Mattias, Matty.*

MAURICE (Latin) Dark-skinned. Variations: *Maurey, Mauricio, Maurie, Mauris, Maurise, Maurizio, Maury, Morey, Morice, Morie, Moris, Moriss, Morrice, Morrie, Morris, Morriss, Morry.*

MAXIMILIAN (Latin) Greatest. Variations: *Maksim, Maksimka, Maksum, Massimiliano, Massimo, Max, Maxi, Maxie, Maxim, Maxime, Maximilano, Maximiliano, Maximillian, Maximino, Maximo, Maximos, Maxy.*

MAXWELL (Scottish) Marcus's well. Variation: *Max.*

MAYER (Latin) Larger. Variations: *Mayor, Meier, Meir, Meirer, Meuer, Myer.*

MAYNARD (English) Hard strength. Variations: *Maynhard, Meinhard, Menard.*

MENACHEM (Hebrew) Comforting. Variations: *Menahem, Mendel.*

MEREDITH (Welsh) Great leader. Variations: *Meredyth, Merideth, Meridith.*

MERLIN (English) Falcon. Merlin actually originated as a name for girls, but the name gradually gravitated to common use for males. Variations: *Meril, Merill, Merrel, Merrell, Merril, Meryl.*

MESHACH (Hebrew) Unknown definition.

MICHAEL (Hebrew) Who is like God? Along with Mohammed and John, Michael could be one of the most popular boys' names in the world in any language. The name is liberally scattered through both the Old and New Testaments as well as throughout the Koran. Michael has been at the top of the names list in this country for over four decades. Variations: *Makis, Micah, Micha, Michail, Michak,*

Michal, Michalek, Michau, Micheal, Michel, Michele, Mick, Mickel, Mickey, Mickie, Micky, Miguel, Mihail, Mihailo, Mihkel, Mikaek, Mikael, Mikala, Mike, Mikelis, Mikey, Mikhail, Mikhalis, Mikhos, Mikkel, Mikko, Mischa, Misha, Mitch, Mitchel, Mitchell.

MILO (German) Generous.

MILTON (English) Mill town.

MOHAMMED (Arabic) Greatly praised. If Michael is the most popular name in the United States and many European countries, then Mohammed and its numerous variations is probably the most popular name in Muslim countries, if not actually the world. Mohammed is the name of the prophet of Islam, and the popularity of the name could possibly be explained by an old Muslim proverb: If you have a hundred sons, give them all the name of Mohammed. The name is also becoming hugely popular among African-Americans. Variations: *Ahmad, Amad, Amed, Hamdrem, Hamdum, Hamid, Hammad, Hammed, Humayd, Mahmed, Mahmoud,*

Mahmud, Mehemet, Mehmet, Mohamad, Mohamed, Mohamet, Mohammad, Muhammad.

MONTEL (English) Unknown definition. Talk-show host Montel Williams probably provided most Americans with their first exposure to this name.

MORGAN (Welsh) Great and bright. Variations: *Morgen, Morrgan.*

MOSES (Hebrew) Arrived by water. Variations: *Moise, Moises, Moisey, Mose, Mosese, Mosha, Moshe, Moss, Moyse, Moze, Mozes.*

MURDOCH (Scottish) Sailor. Variations: *Murdo, Murdock, Murtagh.*

MURRAY (Scottish) Mariner. Murray is another one of those great last-names-as-first-names that is perfect for rejuvenation now. Variations: *Murrey, Murry.*

MYERS (English) One who lives in a swamp. Variation: *Myer.*

MYRON (Greek) Aromatic oil. Variations: *Miron, Myreon.*

NAJIB (Arabic) Smart. Variations: *Nagib, Najeeb.*

NATHAN (Hebrew) Gift from God. Nathan was the name of a prophet who appeared in the Old Testament book of II Samuel, and it's been around ever since. Nathan is a pretty common name in Great Britain and Australia, as well as in the United States. Variations: *Nat, Natan, Nataniele, Nate, Nathanial, Nathaniel, Nathen, Nathon, Natt, Natty.*

NAVEED (Hindu) Good thoughts.

NEHRU (East Indian) Canal.

NEIL (Irish) Champion. Neil is an easygoing name; its original spelling is Niall. Variations: *Neal, Neale, Neall, Nealle, Nealon, Neile, Neill, Neille, Neils, Nels, Niadh, Nial, Niall, Nialle, Niel, Niels, Nigel, Niles, Nilo.*

NELSON (English) Son of Neil. Variations: *Nealson, Neilson, Nilson, Nilsson*.

NEVILLE (French) New town. Variations: *Nevil, Nevile, Nevill, Nevyle*.

NEWELL (English) New hall. Variations: *Newall, Newel, Newhall*.

NEWTON (English) New town.

NICHOLAS (Greek) People of victory. Nicholas was first mentioned in the book of Acts, and the Biblical figure was followed by Saint Nicholas, who is considered to be the patron saint of children (and eventually transmogrified into Santa Claus). Variations: *Nic, Niccolo, Nichol, Nick, Nickolas, Nickolaus, Nicky, Nicol, Nicolaas, Nicolai, Nicolas, Nikita, Nikki, Nikky, Niklas, Niklos, Niko, Nikolai, Nikolais, Nikolas, Nikolaus, Nikolo, Nikolos, Nikos, Nikula*.

NIGEL (Irish) Champion. Variation of Neil. Variations: *Nigal, Nigiel, Nigil*.

NISHAD (Hindu) Seventh note of a scale.

NOAH (Hebrew) Rest. Every little kid knows who Noah is, and so do an increasing number of parents who are choosing this name for their baby boys. Of course, any child with this name should expect the requisite ribbing: where's your Ark? Variations: *Noach, Noak, Noe, Noi, Noy.*

NOAM (Hebrew) Delight.

NOEL (French) Christmas. Variations: *Natal, Natale, Nowel, Nowell.*

NOLAN (Irish) Little proud one. Variations: *Noland, Nolen, Nolin, Nollan, Nuallan.*

NORMAN (English) Northerner. The name Norman originated from the French tribe in Normandy which is most famous for invading England in the year 1066. Variations: *Norm, Normand, Normando, Normen, Normie.*

NORRIS (English) Northerner. Variations: *Noris, Norreys, Norrie, Norriss, Norry.*

NORTON (English) Northern town.

NURI (Arabic) Light. Variations: *Noori, Nur, Nuria, Nuriel, Nury.*

OAKLEY (English) Meadow of oak trees. Variations: *Oaklee, Oakleigh, Oakly.*

OBADIAH (Hebrew) Servant of God. Variations: *Obadias, Obe, Obed, Obediah, Obie, Ovadiach, Ovadiah.*

OBERON (German) Noble and bearlike. Variations: *Auberon, Auberron.*

OBI (African: Nigerian) Heart.

OCTAVIUS (Latin) Eighth child. Variations: *Octave, Octavian, Octavien, Octavio, Octavo, Ottavio.*

OGDEN (English) Valley of oak trees. Variations: *Ogdan, Ogdon.*

OLAF (Scandinavian) Forefather.

OLEG (Russian) Holy. Variation: *Olezka.*

OLIVER (Latin) Olive tree. Variations: *Oliverio, Olivero, Olivier, Olivor, Olley, Ollie, Olliver, Ollivor.*

OMAR (Hebrew) Eloquent. Persian poet Omar Khayyam has lent world-wide exposure to this name. Variations: *Omarr, Omer.*

OREN (Hebrew) Ash tree. Variations: *Orin, Orrin.*

ORION (Greek) Son of fire or light; sunrise. Mythological son of Poseidon.

ORLANDO (Italian) Famous land. Variations: *Ordando, Orland, Orlande, Orlo.*

ORRICK (English) Old oak tree. Variation: *Orric.*

ORSON (Latin) Bearlike. Variations: *Orsen, Orsin, Orsini, Orsino.*

ORTON (English) Shore town.

ORVILLE (French) Golden town. Variations: *Orv, Orval, Orvell, Orvelle, Orvil.*

OSAKWE (African: Nigerian) God agrees.

OSCAR (English) Divine spear. Variations: *Oskar, Osker, Ossie.*

OSMAN (Polish) God protects.

OSWALD (English) Divine power. Variations: *Ossie, Osvald, Oswaldo, Oswall, Oswell.*

OTIS (English) Son of Otto.

OTTO (German) Wealthy. Otto is popular all over the world, including in Hungary, Germany, Sweden, and Russia. Variations: *Odo, Otello, Othello, Otho, Othon, Oto, Ottomar.*

OWEN (Welsh) Well born. Owen could easily be considered a second cousin to the name Evan. Variations: *Owain, Owin.*

OXFORD (English) Oxen crossing a river.

PAGE (French) Intern. Variation: *Paige.*

PALMER (English) Carrying palm branches. Palmer is quickly catching on as a popular first name for both boys and girls. Variations: *Pallmer, Palmar.*

PARIS (English) The city. Variation: *Parris.*

PARKER (English) Park keeper. Variations: *Park, Parke, Parkes, Parks.*

PARNELL (French) Little Peter. Variations: *Parkin, Parnel, Parrnell.*

PARRISH (English) County; church area. Variation: *Parish.*

PASCAL (French) Easter child. Variations: *Pascale, Pascalle, Paschal, Pascoe, Pascow, Pasqual, Pasquale.*

PATRICK (Irish) Noble man. Today, parents who have absolutely no ethnic connection to Ireland are choosing the name Patrick for their sons. Saint Patrick, the patron saint of Ireland, has been popular all over the world for the last two centuries. Variations: *Paddey, Paddie, Paddy, Padraic, Padraig, Padruig, Pat, Patek, Patric,*

Patrice, Patricio, Patricius, Patrik, Patrizio, Patrizius, Patryk.

PATTON (English) Soldier's town. Variations: *Paten, Patin, Paton, Patten, Pattin.*

PAUL (Latin) Small. Variations: *Pablo, Pal, Pali, Palika, Pall, Paolo, Pasha, Pashenka, Pashka, Paska, Paulin, Paulino, Paulis, Paulo, Pauls, Paulus, Pauly, Pavel, Pavils, Pavlicek, Pavlik, Pavlo, Pavlousek, Pawel, Pawl, Pol, Poul.*

PAXTON (English) Peaceful town. Variations: *Packston, Pax, Paxon, Paxten.*

PAYNE (Latin) Countryman. Variation: *Paine.*

PEARSON (English) Son of Piers. Variation: *Pierson.*

PELEKE (Hawaiian) Wise counselor. Variation: *Ferede.*

PEMBROKE (Irish) Cliff. Variation: *Pembrook.*

PERCY (English) Valley prisoner. Variations: *Pearce, Pearcey, Pearcy, Percey.*

PERRY (English) Traveler.

PETER (Greek) Rock. Peter has never been a trendy name; it's rock-solid like its definition. Variations: *Pearce, Pears, Pearson, Pearsson, Peat, Peder, Pedro, Peers, Peet, Peeter, Peirce, Petey, Petie, Petras, Petro, Petronio, Petros, Petter, Pierce, Piero, Pierre, Pierrot, Pierrson, Piers, Pierson, Piet, Pieter, Pietro, Piotr, Pyotr.*

PEYTON (English) Soldier's estate. Variation: *Payton.*

PHELAN (Irish) Wolf.

PHILIP (Greek) Lover of horses. Philip was also one of the original 12 apostles in the Bible. Variations: *Felipe, Felipino, Fil, Filib, Filip, Filipo, Filippo, Fillipek, Fillipp, Fillips, Phil, Philippel, Phill, Phillip, Phillipe, Phillipos, Phillipp, Phillippe, Phillips, Pilib, Pippy.*

PHINEAS (Hebrew) Oracle. Variation: *Pinchas.*

PHOENIX (Greek) Immortal. Variation: *Phenix.*

PICKFORD (English) Ford at a peak.

PITNEY (English) Island of a headstrong man. Variation: *Pittney.*

PLACIDO (Spanish) Peaceful. Variations: *Placid, Placidus, Placyd, Placydo.*

PORTER (Latin) Gatekeeper.

POWELL (English) Last name. Variation: *Powel.*

PRENTICE (English) Apprentice. Variations: *Pren, Prent, Prentis, Prentiss.*

PRESCOTT (English) Priest's cottage. Variations: *Prescot, Prestcot, Prestcott.*

PRESTON (English) Priest's town.

PRICE (Welsh) The son of an ardent man. Variation: *Pryce.*

PRINCE (Latin) Prince. Variations: *Prinz, Prinze.*

PRYOR (Latin) Leader of the monastery. Variation: *Prior.*

PUTNAM (English) One who lives near a pond.

QUENTIN (Latin) Fifth. Variations: *Quent, Quenten, Quenton, Quint, Quinten, Quintin, Quinton, Quito.*

QUIGLEY (Irish) One with messy hair.

QUILLAN (Irish) Cub. Variation: *Quillen.*

QUIMBY (Norse) A woman's house. Variations: *Quenby, Quim, Quin, Quinby.*

QUINCY (French) The estate of the fifth son. Variation: *Quincey.*

QUINLAN (Irish) Strong man. Variations: *Quindlen, Quinley, Quinlin, Quinly.*

QUINN (Irish) Wise. Variation: *Quin.*

QUINTO (Spanish) Home ruler. Variation: *Quiqui.*

RACHIM (Hebrew) Compassion. Variations: *Racham, Rachmiel, Raham, Rahim.*

RADCLIFF (English) Red cliff. Variations: *Radcliffe, Radclyffe.*

RAFI (Arabic) Exalted.

RALEIGH (English) Deer meadow. Variations: *Rawleigh, Rawley, Rawly.*

RALPH (English) Wolf-counselor. Variations: *Ralphie, Raoul, Raul, Raulas, Raulo, Rolf, Rolph.*

RANDOLPH (English) Wolf with a shield. Variations: *Randal, Randall, Randel, Randell, Randey, Randie, Randil, Randle, Randol, Randolf, Randy.*

RAOUL (French) Variation of Ralph. Variation: *Raul.*

RAPHAEL (Hebrew) God has healed. Variations: *Rafael, Rafel, Rafello, Raffaello.*

RASHID (Turkish) Righteous. Variations: *Rasheed, Rasheid, Rasheyd.*

RAYMOND (German) Counselor and protector. Saint Raymond is considered to be the patron saint of lawyers. Variations: *Raimondo, Raimund, Raimunde, Raimundo, Rajmund, Ramon, Ramond,*

Ramone, Ray, Rayment, Raymonde, Raymondo, Raymund, Raymunde, Raymundo, Reimond.

REDMOND (Irish) Counselor. Variation of Raymond. Variations: *Radmond, Radmund, Redmund.*

REECE (Welsh) Fiery, zealous. Variations: *Rees, Reese, Rhys.*

REGINALD (English) Strong counselor. Variations: *Reg, Reggie, Reginalt.*

REMINGTON (English) Family of ravens. Variations: *Rem, Remee, Remi, Remie, Remmy.*

RENNY (Irish) Small and mighty.

REUBEN (Hebrew) Behold a son. Variations: *Reuban, Reubin, Reuven, Reuvin, Rube, Ruben, Rubin, Rubu.*

REX (Latin) King.

REYNOLD (English) Powerful adviser. Variations: *Ranald, Renald, Renaldo, Renauld, Renault, Reynaldo, Reynaldos, Reynolds, Rinaldo.*

RICHARD (German) Strong ruler. Variations: *Dic, Dick, Dickie, Dicky, Ricard, Ricardo, Riccardo, Ricciardo, Rich, Richardo, Richards, Richart, Richerd, Richi, Richie, Rick, Rickard, Rickert, Rickey, Rickie, Ricky, Rico, Rihards, Riki, Riks, Riocard, Riqui, Risa, Ritch, Ritchard, Ritcherd, Ritchie, Ritchy, Rostik, Rostislav, Rostya, Ryszard.*

RICHMOND (French) Lush mountain.

RIDGLEY (English) Meadow on a ridge. Variations: *Ridgeleigh, Ridgeley, Ridglea, Ridglee, Ridgleigh.*

RIDLEY (English) Red meadow. Variations: *Riddley, Ridlea, Ridleigh, Ridly.*

RILEY (Irish) Brave. Variations: *Reilly, Ryley.*

RIORDAN (Irish) Minstrel. Variations: *Rearden, Reardon.*

RIPLEY (English) Shouting man's meadow. Variations: *Ripleigh, Riply, Ripp.*

ROBERT (English) Bright fame. Robert is one of the most popular names in the world, especially in the United States. It has endless variations in every language, and one theory holds that so many men were named Robert from the time of the Middle Ages up until today that many variants were necessary so that people could distinguish one Robert from another. Variations: *Bob, Bobbey, Bobbie, Bobby, Riobard, Rob, Robb, Robbi, Robbie, Robbin, Robby, Robbyn, Rober, Robers, Roberto, Roberts, Robi, Robin, Robinet, Robyn, Rubert, Ruberto, Rudbert, Ruperto, Ruprecht.*

RODERICK (German) Famous ruler. Variations: *Rod, Rodd, Roddie, Roddy, Roderic, Roderich, Roderigo, Rodique, Rodrich, Rodrick, Rodrigo, Rodrique, Rurich, Rurik.*

RODMAN (English) Famous man.

RODNEY (English) Island clearing. Variations: *Rodnee, Rodnie, Rodny.*

ROGER (German) Renowned spearman. Variations: *Rodger, Rogelio, Rogerio, Rogerios, Rogers, Ruggerio, Ruggero, Rutger, Ruttger.*

ROLAND (German) Famous land. Variations: *Rolle, Rolli, Rollie, Rollin, Rollins, Rollo, Rollon, Rolly, Rolo, Rolon, Row, Rowe, Rowland, Rowlands, Rowlandson.*

ROMAN (Latin) One from Rome. Variations: *Romain, Romano, Romanos, Romulo, Romulos, Romulus.*

RONALD (English) Powerful adviser. Variations: *Ranald, Ron, Ronn, Ronney, Ronni, Ronnie, Ronny.*

ROOSEVELT (Dutch) Field of roses.

ROSARIO (Portuguese) The rosary.

ROSCOE (Scandinavian) Deer forest.

ROSS (Scottish) Cape. Variations: *Rosse, Rossie, Rossy.*

ROWAN (Irish) Red. Variation: *Rowen.*

ROY (Irish) Red.

ROYCE (American) Roy's son. Variations: *Roice, Royse.*

RUFUS (Latin) Red-haired. Variations: *Ruffus, Rufo, Rufous.*

RUPERT (German) Bright fame. Variation of Robert. Variations: *Ruperto, Ruprecht.*

RUSSELL (French) Red-haired. Variations: *Rus, Russ, Russel.*

RUSTY (French) Red-haired. Variation: *Rustie.*

RYAN (Irish) Last name. Variations: *Ryne, Ryon, Ryun.*

RYLAND (English) Land of rye. Variation: *Ryeland.*

RYSZARD (Polish) Brave ruler. Variant of Richard.

SABIR (Arabic) Patient. Variation: *Sabri*.

SADIKI (African: Swahili) Faithful.

SAEED (African: Swahili) Happy.

SAID (Arabic) Happy. Variations: *Saeed, Saied, Saiyid, Sayeed, Sayid, Syed*.

SALVATORE (Latin) Savior. Variations: *Sal, Salvador, Salvator*.

SAMIR (Arabic) Entertainer.

SAMUEL (Hebrew) God listens. Samuel has tended to be popular over the last 100 years or so. Variations: *Sam, Sammie, Sammy, Samouel, Samuele, Samuello*.

SANBORN (English) Sandy river. Variations: *Sanborne, Sanbourn, Sanburn, Sanburne, Sandborn, Sandbourne*.

SANTIAGO (Spanish) Saint.

SAUL (Hebrew) Asked for.

SAWYER (English) Woodworker. Variations: *Sayer, Sayers, Sayre, Sayres.*

SCHUYLER (Dutch) Shield. Variations: *Schuylar, Skuyler, Skylar, Skyler.*

SCOTT (English) One from Scotland. Variations: *Scot, Scottie, Scotto, Scotty.*

SEAN (Irish) God is good. Variation of John. Variations: *Seann, Shaine, Shane, Shaughn, Shaun, Shawn, Shayn, Shayne.*

SEBASTIAN (Latin) One from Sebastia, an ancient Roman city. Variations: *Seb, Sebastien, Sebbie.*

SERGE (Latin) Servant. Variations: *Serg, Sergei, Sergey, Sergi, Sergie, Sergio, Sergius.*

SETH (Hebrew) To appoint. Seth was the third son of Adam and Eve and was born after the death of his older siblings, Cain and Abel.

SEYMOUR (French) From St. Maur, a village in France. Variations: *Seamor, Seamore, Seamour, Si, Sy.*

SHAFER (Hebrew) Handsome.

SHALOM (Hebrew) Peace. Variation: *Sholom*.

SHAMIR (Hebrew) Flint. Variation: *Shamur*.

SHAQUILLE (African-American) Newly created.

SHARIF (Hindu) Respected. Variations: *Shareef*, *Shereef*, *Sherif*.

SHELBY (English) Village on the ledge. Variations: *Shelbey*, *Shelbie*.

SHEPHERD (English) Sheepherder. Variations: *Shep*, *Shepard*, *Shephard*, *Shepp*, *Sheppard*, *Shepperd*.

SHERWOOD (English) Shining forest. Variations: *Sherwoode*, *Shurwood*.

SHILOH (Hebrew) Unknown definition. Variation: *Shilo*.

SIDNEY (English) One from Sidney, a town in France. Variations: *Sid*, *Siddie*, *Sidon*, *Sidonio*, *Syd*, *Sydney*.

SIMON (Hebrew) God hears. Variations: *Simeon, Simion, Simm, Simms, Simone, Symms, Symon.*

SNOWDEN (English) Snowy mountain. Variation: *Snowdon.*

SOCRATES (Greek) Named for the Greek philosopher. Variations: *Socratis, Sokrates.*

SOLOMON (Hebrew) Peaceable. Variations: *Salamen, Salamon, Salamun, Salaun, Salman, Salmon, Salom, Salomo, Salomon, Salomone, Selim, Shelomoh, Shlomo, Sol, Solaman, Sollie, Solly, Soloman, Solomo, Solomonas, Solomone.*

SPALDING (English) Divided field. Variation: *Spaulding.*

SPENCER (English) Seller of goods. Variations: *Spence, Spense, Spenser.*

STANLEY (English) Stony meadow. Variation: *Stan, Stanlea, Stanlee, Stanleigh, Stanly.*

STAVROS (Greek) Crowned.

STEADMAN (English) One who lives on a farm. Variations: *Steadmann, Stedman.*

STEPHEN (Greek) Crowned. Variations: *Stefan, Stefano, Stefanos, Stefans, Steffan, Steffel, Steffen, Stefos, Stepa, Stepan, Stepanek, Stepek, Stephan, Stephane, Stephanos, Stephanus, Stephens, Stephenson, Stepka, Stepousek, Stevan, Steve, Steven, Stevenson, Stevie.*

STEWART (English) Steward. Variations: *Stew, Steward, Stu, Stuart.*

SULLIVAN (Irish) Black-eyed. Variations: *Sullavan, Sullevan, Sulliven.*

SUMANTRA (Hindu) Good advice.

SUTTON (English) Southern town.

SYLVESTER (Latin) Forested. Variations: *Silvester, Silvestre, Silvestro, Sly.*

TAGGART (Irish) Son of a priest.

TALBOT (English) Last name. Variations: *Talbert, Talbott, Tallbot, Tallbott.*

TANAY (Hindu) Son.

TANNER (English) One who tans leather. Variations: *Tan, Tanier, Tann, Tanney, Tannie, Tanny.*

TATE (English) Happy. Variations: *Tait, Taitt, Tayte.*

TAYLOR (English) Tailor. Taylor may soon become the sole property of girls. Tyler is a good alternative for boys. Variations: *Tailer, Tailor, Tayler, Taylour.*

TEMPLETON (English) Town near the temple. Variations: *Temple, Templeten.*

TENNESEE (Native American: Cherokee) The state.

TERENCE (Latin) Roman clan name. Variations: *Tarrance, Terencio, Terrance, Terrence, Terrey, Terri, Terry.*

TERRILL (German) Follower of Thor. Variations: *Terrall, Terrel, Terrell, Terryl, Terryll, Tirrell, Tyrrell.*

THADDEUS (Aramaic) Brave. Variations: *Taddeo, Tadeo, Tadio, Thad, Thaddaus.*

THANOS (Greek) Royal. Variation: *Thanasis.*

THATCHER (English) Roof thatcher. Variations: *Thacher, Thatch, Thaxter.*

THEODORE (Greek) Gift from God. Variations: *Teador, Ted, Tedd, Teddey, Teddie, Teddy, Tedor, Teodor, Teodoro, Theo, Theodor.*

THEOPHILUS (Greek) Loved by God. Variations: *Teofil, Theophile.*

THOMAS (Aramaic) Twin. Saint Thomas was the impetus for this name's popularity around the time of the Middle Ages. Variations: *Tam, Tameas, Thom, Thoma, Thompson, Thomson, Thumas, Thumo, Tom, Tomas, Tomaso, Tomasso, Tomaz, Tomcio, Tomek, Tomelis, Tomi, Tomie, Tomislaw, Tomm, Tommy, Tomsen, Tomson, Toomas, Tuomas, Tuomo.*

THORNTON (English) Thorny town.

THURSTON (Scandinavian) Thor's stone. Variations: *Thorstan, Thorstein, Thorsteinn, Thorsten, Thurstain, Thurstan, Thursten, Torstein, Torsten, Torston.*

TIERNAN (Irish) Little lord. Variations: *Tierney, Tighearnach, Tighearnan.*

TIMOTHY (Greek) Honoring God. Variations: *Tim, Timmothy, Timmy, Timo, Timofeo, Timon, Timoteo, Timothe, Timotheo, Timotheus, Timothey, Tymmothy, Tymothy.*

TITUS (Latin) Unknown definition. Variations: *Tito, Titos.*

TODD (English) Fox. Variation: *Tod.*

TONY (Latin) Nickname for Anthony that has evolved into its own freestanding name. Variations: *Toney, Tonie.*

TRACY (French) Area in France. Variations: *Trace, Tracey, Treacy.*

TRAVIS (French) Toll-taker. Variations: *Traver, Travers, Travus, Travys.*

TRENT (Latin) Rushing waters. Variations: *Trenten, Trentin, Trenton.*

TREVOR (Welsh) Large homestead. Variations: *Trefor, Trev, Trevar, Trever, Trevis.*

TREY (English) Three.

TRISTAN (Welsh) Famous Welsh folklore character. Variations: *Tris, Tristam.*

TURNER (English) Woodworker.

TWAIN (English) Split in two. Variations: *Twaine, Twayn.*

TYLER (English) Tile maker. Tyler became an extremely popular name in the '90s for both boys and girls, though it is more widely used for boys. Variations: *Ty, Tylar.*

TYRONE (Irish) Land of Owen. Variations: *Tiron, Tirone, Ty, Tyron.*

TYSON (English) Firebrand. Variations: *Tieson, Tison, Tysen.*

TZACH (Hebrew) Clean. Variations: *Tzachai, Tzachar.*

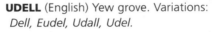

UDELL (English) Yew grove. Variations: *Dell, Eudel, Udall, Udel.*

ULYSSES (Latin) Wrathful. Variation of Odysseus. Variations: *Ulises, Ulisse.*

UMBERTO (Italian) Famous German. Variation of Humbert.

UPTON (English) Hill town.

URI (Hebrew) God's light. Variations: *Uria, Uriah, Urias, Urie, Uriel.*

VAIL (English) City in Colorado.
Variations: *Vaile, Vale, Vayle.*

VALENTINE (Latin) Strong.
Variations: *Val, Valentin, Valentino, Valentyn.*

VALMIKI (Hindu) Ant hill.

VANCE (English) Swamp land. Variations: *Van, Vancelo, Vann.*

VANDYKE (Dutch) From the dyke. Variation: *Van Dyck.*

VANYA (Russian) God is good. Variation of John. Variations: *Vanek, Vanka.*

VARICK (German) Defending ruler. Variation: *Varrick.*

VAUGHN (Welsh) Small. Variation: *Vaughan.*

VERNON (French) Alder tree. Variations: *Vern, Verne.*

VICTOR (Latin) Conqueror. Variations: *Vic, Vick, Victoir, Victorien, Victorino, Victorio, Viktor, Vitenka, Vitor, Vittore, Vittorio, Vittorios.*

VINCENT (Latin) To conquer. Variations: *Vikent, Vikenti, Vikesha, Vin, Vince, Vincente, Vincenz, Vincenzio, Vincenzo, Vinci, Vinco, Vinn, Vinnie, Vinny.*

VITO (Latin) Alive. Variations: *Vital, Vitale, Vitalis.*

VITUS (French) Forest. Variation: *Vitya.*

VLADIMIR (Slavic) Famous prince. Variations: *Vlad, Vladamir, Vladimeer, Vladko, Vladlen.*

WADE (English) To cross a river.

WADSWORTH (English) Village near a river crossing. Variation: *Waddsworth.*

WAGNER (German) Wagon maker. Variation: *Waggoner.*

WAITE (English) Watchman.
Variations: *Waits, Wayte.*

WALDEN (English) Forested valley.
Some parents will choose it out of
deference to Henry David Thoreau
and Walden Pond. Variation:
Waldon.

WALDO (German) Strong.

WALKER (English) One who walks on cloth. Last name.

WALTER (German) Ruler of the people. Variations:
Walt, Walther, Waltr, Watkin.

WALTON (English) Walled town.

WARREN (German) Protector friend. Variations:
Warrin, Warriner.

WASHINGTON (English) Town of smart men.

WAYNE (English) Wagon maker. Version of
Wainwright. Variations: *Wain, Wainwright, Wayn,
Waynwright.*

WEBSTER (English) Weaver. Variations: *Web, Webb, Weber.*

WENDELL (German) Wanderer. Variations: *Wendel, Wendle.*

WESLEY (English) Western meadow. Two brothers, John and Charles Wesley, were the founders of the Methodist church in England. Variations: *Wes, Wesly, Wessley, Westleigh, Westley.*

WESTON (English) Western town. Variations: *Westen, Westin.*

WHARTON (English) Town on a river bank. Variation: *Warton.*

WHEATLEY (English) Wheat field. Variations: *Wheatlea, Wheatleigh, Wheatlie, Wheatly.*

WHEELER (English) Wheel maker.

WHITCOMB (English) White valley. Variation: *Whitcombe.*

WHITELAW (English) White hill. Variation: *Whitlaw.*

WHITFIELD (English) White field.

WHITLOCK (English) White lock of hair.

WHITNEY (English) White island.

WILBUR (German) Brilliant. Variations: *Wilber, Wilbert, Wilburt, Willbur.*

WILEY (English) Water meadow. Variations: *Willey, Wylie.*

WILLIAM (German) Constant protector. William is one of the most popular names throughout English-speaking countries. Variations: *Bill, Billie, Billy, Guillaume, Guillaums, Guillermo, Vas, Vasilak, Vasilious, Vaska, Vassos, Vila, Vildo, Vilek, Vilem, Vilhelm, Vili, Viliam, Vilkl, Ville, Vilmos, Vilous, Will, Willem, Willi, Williamson, Willie, Willil, Willis, Willy, Wilson, Wilhelm.*

WILSON (English) Son of Will. Variation: *Willson.*

WOLFGANG (German) Wolf fight.

WOODROW (English) Row in the woods. Variations: *Wood, Woody.*

WYATT (French) Little fighter. Variations: *Wiatt, Wyat.*

WYNN (English) Friend. Variations: *Win, Winn, Wynne.*

XAVIER (English) New house. Variations: *Saverio, Xaver.*

XENOS (Greek) Guest. Variations: *Xeno, Zenos.*

YAKIM (Hebrew) God develops. Variation: *Jakim.*

YALE (English) Up on the hill.

YANCY (Native American) Englishman. Variations: *Yance, Yancey, Yantsey.*

YANNIS (Greek) God is good. Variation of John. Variations: *Yannakis, Yanni, Yiannis.*

YARDLEY (English) Enclosed meadow. Variations: *Yardlea, Yardlee, Yardleigh, Yardly.*

YATES (English) Gates. Variation: *Yeats.*

YEHUDI (Hebrew) Praise. Variations: *Yechudi, Yechudil, Yehuda, Yehudah.*

YERIK (Russian) God is exalted. Variation of Jeremiah. Variation: *Yeremey.*

YO (Chinese) Bright.

YONG (Chinese) Brave.

YORK (English) Yew tree. Variations: *Yorick, Yorke, Yorrick.*

YOSEF (Hebrew) God increases. Variations: *Yoseff, Yosif, Yousef, Yusef, Yusif, Yusuf, Yuzef.*

YOSHI (Japanese) Quiet.

YULE (English) Christmas.

YUMA (Native American) Son of the chief.

YUSUF (Arabic) God will increase. Variations: *Youssef, Yousuf, Yusef, Yusif, Yussef.*

YVES (French) Yew wood. Variation: *Yvon.*

ZACHARIAH (Hebrew) The Lord has remembered. Zachariah and its many variations is one of the more popular names around today. Variations: *Zacaria, Zacarias, Zach, Zacharia, Zacharias, Zacharie, Zachary, Zachery, Zack, Zackariah, Zackerias, Zackery, Zak, Zakarias, Zakarie, Zako, Zeke.*

ZAFAR (Arabic) To win. Variation: *Zafir.*

ZAHID (Arabic) Strict.

ZAHIR (Hebrew) Bright. Variations: *Zaheer, Zahur.*

ZALE (Greek) Strength from the sea. Variation: *Zayle.*

ZAMIR (Hebrew) Song.

ZANE (English) God is good. Variation of John. Variations: *Zain, Zayne.*

ZARED (Hebrew) Trap.

ZEBULON (Hebrew) To exalt. Variations: *Zebulen, Zebulun.*

ZEDEKIAH (Hebrew) God is just. Variations: *Tzedekia, Tzidkiya, Zed, Zedechiah, Zedekia, Zedekias.*

ZEHARIAH (Hebrew) Light of God. Variations: *Zeharia, Zeharya.*

ZEKE (Hebrew) The strength of God. Zeke got its start as a nickname for Ezekiel, and gradually came into its own as an independent name.

ZEPHANIAH (Hebrew) Protection. Variations: *Zeph, Zephan.*

ZEUS (Greek) Living. King of the gods. Variations: *Zeno, Zenon, Zinon.*

ZINDEL (Hebrew) Protector of mankind. Variation: *Zindil.*

ZOWIE (Greek) Life.

Girls' Names

ABEY (Native American: Omaha) Leaf.

ABIGAIL (Hebrew) Father's joy. In the Bible, Abigail was the name of King David's wife. Abigail was the name of the wife of President John Adams and the mother of President John Quincy Adams. Variations: *Abagael, Abagail, Abagale, Abbey, Abbi, Abbie, Abbigael, Abbigail, Abbigale, Abby, Abbye, Abbygael, Abbygail, Abbygale, Abigale, Abigayle, Avigail.*

ADORA (Latin) Much adored. Variations: *Adoree, Adoria, Adorlee, Dora, Dori, Dorie, Dorrie.*

ADRIANE (German) Black earth. This pretty name is growing in popularity. Variations: *Adriana, Adriane, Adrianna, Adriannah, Adrianne, Adrien, Adriena, Adrienah, Adrienne.*

AGATHA (Greek) Good. Agatha is the patron saint of firefighters and nurses. Variations: *Aga, Agace, Agacia, Agafia, Agasha, Agata, Agate, Agathe, Agathi, Agatta, Ageneti, Aggi, Aggie, Aggy, Akeneki.*

AISHA (Arabic) Life. Variations: *Aishah, Aisia, Aisiah, Asha, Ashah, Ashia, Ashiah, Asia, Asiah, Ayeesa, Ayeesah, Ayeesha, Ayeeshah, Ayeisa.*

AKIBA (African) Unknown definition.

ALEXANDRA (Greek) One who defends. Feminine version of Alexander. The name has been long associated with the royalty. Variations: *Alejandrina, Aleka, Aleksasha, Aleksey, Aleksi, Alesia, Aleska, Alessandra, Alessa, Alessi, Alex, Alexa, Alexanderia, Alexanderina, Alexena, Alexene, Alexi, Alexia, Alexie, Alexina, Alexiou, Alexis.*

ALICIA (English, Hispanic, Swedish) Truthful. Variations: *Alesha, Alesia, Alisha, Alissa, Alycia, Alysha, Alyshia, Alysia, Ilysha.*

ALISON (German) Diminutive version of Alice. Variations: *Alisann, Alisanne, Alisoun, Alisun, Allcen, Allcenne, Allicen, Allicenne, Allie, Allisann, Allisanne, Allison, Allisoun, Ally, Allysann, Allysanne, Allyson, Alyeann, Alysanne, Alyson.*

ALTHEA (Greek) With the potential to heal. Variations: *Altha, Althaia, Altheta, Althia.*

ANGELA (Greek) Messenger of God, angel. Variations: *Aingeal, Ange, Angel, Angele, Angelene, Angelia, Angelica, Angelika, Angelina, Angeline, Angelique, Angelita, Angie, Angiola, Anjelica, Anngilla.*

ANN (English) Grace. Ann, along with its many variations, has long been one of the most commonly used names Variations: *Ana, Anita, Anitra, Anitte, Anna, Annah, Anne, Annie, Annita, Annitra, Annitta, Hannah, Hannelore.*

APRIL (English) Named for the month. Variations:

Abrial, Abril, Aprilete, Aprilette, Aprili, Aprille, Apryl, Averil, Avril.

ARABELLA (English) In prayer. Variations: *Arabel, Arabela, Arbell, Arbella, Bel, Bella, Belle, Orabella, Orbella.*

ARIANA (Welsh) Silver. Variations: *Ariane, Arianie, Arianna, Arianne.*

ARIEL (Hebrew) Lioness of God. Ariel was a water sprite as well as a male sprite in Shakespeare's *Tempest.* Variations: *Aeriel, Aeriela, Ari, Ariela, Ariella, Arielle, Ariellel.*

ASHLEY (English) Ash tree. Ashley started out as a boys' name, with Ashley Wilkes from *Gone with the Wind* popularizing the name. But from that point on, Ashley seemed destined to be a girls' name. Variations: *Ashely, Ashla, Ashlan, Ashlea, Ashlee, Ashleigh, Ashlie, Ashly, Ashton.*

AUDREY (English) Nobility and strength. Variations: *Audey, Audi, Audie, Audra, Audre, Audree, Audreen, Audri, Audria, Audrie, Audry, Audrye, Audy.*

AUGUSTA (Latin) Majestic. Feminine version of August and Augustus. Variations: *Agusta, Augustia, Augustina,*

Augustine, Augustyna, Augustyne, Austina, Austine, Austyna, Austyne.

AURORA (Latin) Roman goddess of dawn. Variation: *Aurore.*

AVERY (English) Elf advisor. Avery fits the latest baby-naming trends perfectly, since it is unisex as well as a last name.

AYESHA (Persian) Small girl.

AZARIA (Hebrew) Helped by God. Variations: *Azariah, Azelia.*

BAILEY (English) Bailiff. Bailey has become a popular name for both boys and girls in the last decade. Variations: *Bailee, Baylee, Bayley, Baylie.*

BARBARA (Greek) Foreign. Barbara was once one of the most popular names for girls. As part of its legacy, Barbara has left behind lots of variations on a theme: *Babb, Babbett, Babbette, Babe, Babett, Babette, Babita, Babs, Barb, Barbary, Barbe,*

Barbette, Barbey, Barbi, Barbie, Barbra, Barby, Basha, Basia, Vaoka, Varenka, Varina, Varinka, Varka, Varvara, Varya, Vava.

BASIA (Hebrew) Daughter of God. Variations: Basha, Basya.

BEATRICE (Latin) She brings joy. The Beatrice that most American kids know is Beatrix Potter. Variations: Bea, Beatrisa, Beatrise, Beatrix, Beatriz, Beattie, Bebe, Bee, Beitris, Beitriss.

BERNADETTE (French) Brave as a bear. Feminine version of Bernard. Variations: Berna, Bernadene, Bernadett, Bernadina, Bernadine, Bernarda, Bernardina, Bernardine, Bernetta, Bernette, Berni, Bernie, Bernita, Berny.

BETHANY (English) House of poverty; a Biblical village near Jerusalem. Variations: Bethanee, Bethani, Bethanie, BethAnn, Bethann, Bethanne, Bethannie, Bethanny.

BIANCA (Italian) White. Variations: Beanka, Biancha, Bionca, Bionka, Blanca, Blancha.

BLAIR (English) A flat piece of land. In the '50s, Blair was a common name for boys. In the '70s and '80s, Blair turned into a girls' name. Variations: *Blaire, Blayre.*

BREANA (Celtic) Strong. Feminine version of Brian. Variations: *Breann, Breanna, Breanne, Briana, Briane, Briann, Brianna, Brianne, Briona, Bryanna, Bryanne.*

BRIDGET (Irish) Strength. Variations: *Birgit, Birgitt, Birgitte, Breeda, Brid, Bride, Bridgett, Bridgette, Bridgitte, Brigantia, Brighid, Brigid, Brigid, Brigida, Brigit, Brigitt, Brigitta, Brigitte, Brygida, Brygitka.*

BRITTANY (English) Feminine version of Britain. This has been one of the most popular names for girls since the mid-'80s. Variations: *Brinnee, Britany, Britney, Britni, Brittan, Brittaney, Brittani, Brittania, Brittanie, Brittannia, Britteny, Brittni, Brittnie, Brittny.*

BRONWYN (Welsh) Pure of breast. Variation: *Bronwen.*

BROOKE (English) One who lives by a brook. Variation: *Brook.*

CAITLIN (Irish) Pure. Caitlin, created by the combination of Katherine and Lynn, has become a very popular name. Variations: *Caitilin, Caitlan, Caitlion, Caitlon, Caitlyn, Caitlynne, Catlin, Kaitlin, Kaitlyn, Kaitlynn, Kaitlynne, Katelin, Katelynn.*

CAMILLE (French) Assistant in the church. Variations: *Cam, Cama, Camala, Cami, Camila, Camile, Camilia, Camilla, Cammi, Cammie, Cammy, Cammylle, Camyla, Kamila, Kamilka.*

CAROLINE (German) Woman. Feminine version of Carl, as well as Charles in diminutive form. Variations: *Carolenia, Carolin, Carolina, Carolyn, Carolynn, Carolynne, Karolin, Karolina, Karoline, Karolyn, Karolyna, Karolyne, Karolynn, Karolynne.*

CASEY (Irish) Observant. Also common as a boys' name. Out of all the boys' names that become popular as girls' names, Casey may actually be one of the few that remain popular in both camps. Variations: *Cacia, Casee,*

Casie, Cassie, Caycey, Caysey, Kacey, Kacia, Kasee, Kasie, Kaycey, Kaysey.

CASSIDY (Gaelic) Clever. Variations: *Cassidey, Cassidi, Cassidie, Kasady, Kassidey, Kassidi, Kassidie, Kassidy.*

CATHERINE (English) Pure. Variations: *Catalina, Catarina, Catarine, Cateline, Catharin, Catharine, Catharyna, Catharyne, Cathe, Cathee, Cathelin, Cathelina, Cathelle, Catherin, Catherina, Cathi, Cathie, Cathy, Catrin, Catrina, Catrine, Catryna, Caty.*

CECELIA (Latin) Blind. Feminine version of Cecil. Variations: *C'Ceal, Cacilia, Cecely, Ceci, Cecia, Cecile, Cecilie, Cecille, Cecilyn, Cecyle, Cecylia, Ceil, Cele, Celenia, Celia, Celie, Celina, Celinda, Celine, Celinna, Celle, Cesia, Cespa, Cicely, Cicilia, Cycyl, Sessaley, Seelia, Seelie, Seely, Seslia, Sesseelya, Sessile, Sessilly, Sheelagh, Sheelah, Sheila, Sheilagh, Sheilah, Shela, Shelah, Shelia, Shiela, Sile, Sileas, Siseel, Sisely, Siselya, Sisilya, Sissela, Sissie, Sissy.*

CELESTE (Latin) Heaven. Variations: *Cela, Celesse, Celesta, Celestia, Celestiel, Celestina, Celestine, Celestyn, Celestyna, Celinka, Celisse, Cesia, Inka, Selinka.*

CHANDELLE (African-American) Variations: *Chan, Chandell, Shan, Shandell, Shandelle.*

CHANTAL (French) Rocky area. Variations: *Chantale, Chantalle, Chante, Chantele, Chantelle, Shanta, Shantae, Shantal, Shantalle, Shantay, Shante, Shanteigh, Shantel, Shantell, Shantella, Shantelle, Shontal, Shontalle, Shontelle.*

CHARLA (English) Man. Feminine version of Charles. Variations: *Charlaine, Charlayne, Charlena, Charlene, Charli, Charlie, Charline, Cherlene, Cherline, Sharlayne, Sharleen, Sharlene.*

CHARLOTTE (French) Small beauty. Variant of Charles.

CHELSEA (English) Ship port. Chelsea Clinton gave a huge boost to the visibility of this name in the '90s. Variations: *Chelsa, Chelsee, Chelsey, Chelsi, Chelsie, Chelsy.*

CHERYL (English) Charity. Variations: *Cherill, Cherrill, Cherryl, Cheryle, Cheryll, Sherryll, Sheryl.*

CHEYENNE (Native American: Algonquin) Specific tribe. Cheyenne is a western place name that is bound to become more popular. Variations: *Cheyanna, Cheyanne, Chiana, Chianna*.

CHLOE (Greek) Young blade of grass. Variations: *Clo, Cloe*.

CHRISTINE (English) Anointed one. Feminine version of Christian. Variations: *Chris, Chrissy, Christa, Christen, Christi, Christiana, Christiane, Christiann, Christianna, Christie, Christina, Christy, Teena, Teina, Tena, Tina, Tinah*.

CLARA (English) Bright. Variations: *Clair, Claire, Clairette, Clairine, Clare, Claresta, Clareta, Clarette, Clarice, Clarie, Clarinda, Clarine, Claris, Clarisa, Clarissa, Clarisse, Clarita, Claryce, Clerissa, Clerisse, Cleryce, Clerysse, Klara, Klari, Klarice, Klarissa, Klaryce, Klaryssa*.

COLETTE (French) Triumphant people. Its origin is a variation of the name Nicolette. Variations: *Coletta, Collet, Collete, Collett*.

COURTNEY (English) Dweller in the court, or farm. In the late '80s, Courtney was one of the most popular names given to girls in this country. Variations: *Cortney, Courtenay, Courteney, Courtnie.*

DAKOTA (English) State name; also used for boys. Dakota is currently hot, hot, hot, but that can only mean that it soon will be on the wane.

DANA (English) From Denmark. Dana is quickly becoming popular among both boys and girls, but it is more common as a girls' name. Variations: *Daina, Danay, Danaye, Dane, Danee, Danet, Danna, Dayna, Denae.*

DAPHNE (Greek) Ancient mythological nymph who was transformed into a laurel tree. Variations: *Dafne, Daphney, Daphny.*

DARIA (Greek) Luxurious. Variations: *Darian, Darianna, Dariele, Darielle, Darienne, Darrelle.*

DARLENE (English) Darling. Variations: *Darla, Darleane, Darleen, Darleena, Darlena, Darlina, Darline.*

DAWN (English) Sunrise, the dawn. Dawn was a popular name in the late '60s and early '70s. Variations: *Dawna, Dawne, Dawnelle, Dawnetta, Dawnette, Dawnielle, Dawnika, Dawnn.*

DEANDRA (African-American) Newly created name. Variations: *Deanda, Deandrea, Deandria, Deeandra, Dianda, Diandra, Diandre.*

DEBORAH (Hebrew) Bee. Variations: *Deb, Debbi, Debbie, Debby, Debi, Debora, Deborrah, Debra, Debrah, Devora, Devorah, Devra.*

DELIA (Greek) Visible. Variations: *Del, Delise, Delya, Delys, Delyse.*

DELILAH (Hebrew) Delicate. Delilah is perhaps best known as Samson's mistress in the Biblical book of Judges. Variations: *Dalila, Delila.*

DENISE (French) Lame god. Variations: *Denese, Deni, Denice, Deniece, Denisha, Denize, Dennise, Denyce, Denys, Denys.*

DERYN (Welsh) Bird. Variations: *Derren, Derrin, Derrine, Derron, Deryn.*

DESIREE (French) Longing. Though some people see this name as being a bit too adult to tag on a little girl. Its roots stem from Puritanical times, when Desire was the basic name. Variations: *Desarae, Desira, Desyre, Dezarae, Dezirae, Diseraye, Diziree, Dsaree.*

DEVON (English) Region in southern England. Variations: *Devan, Devana, Devanna, Devona, Devondra, Devonna, Devonne, Devyn, Devynn.*

DEWANDA (African-American) Combination of De + Wanda.

DIANA (Latin) Divine. Roman goddess of the moon and of hunting. Variations: *Dee, Diahann, Dian, Diane, Dianna, Dianne, Didi, Dyan, Dyana.*

DIONNE (Greek) Dione is a Greek mythological figure. Dionne is also the feminine version of Dennis, which in turn is formed from the name of another Greek god, Dionysus, the god of wine. Variations: *Deonne, Dion, Diona, Dione, Dionia, Dionna, Dionysia.*

DOMINIQUE (Latin) Lord. Feminine version of Dominick. Currently it is gaining ground in popularity, and its peak seems to be a few years down the road. Variations: *Dominica, Dominika.*

DONNA (Italian) Woman of the home. The name Donna was at its peak of popularity in the '50s and '60s. Variations: *Dahna, Donielle, Donisha, Donetta, Donnalee, Donnalyn, DonnaMarie, Donni, Donnie, Donya.*

DOROTHY (Greek) Gift from God. Variations: *Dollie, Dolly, Dorethea, Doro, Dorotea, Dorotha, Dorothea, Dorothee, Dorothia, Dorrit, Dortha, Dorthea, Dot, Dottie, Dotty.*

EBONY (African-American) Black wood. Ebony is one of the most popular names that African-American parents are giving their daughters these days. Variations: *Ebbony, Eboney, Eboni, Ebonie.*

EDEN (Hebrew) Pleasure. Variations: *Eaden, Eadin, Edena, Edenia Edana, Edin.*

EDWINA (English) Rich friend. Feminine version of Edwin. Variations: *Edween, Edweena, Edwena, Edwiena, Edwuna, Edwyna.*

EILEEN (Irish) Shining, bright. Familiar version of Helen. Eileen has been extremely popular among families of Irish heritage. Variations: *Aileen, Ailene, Alene, Aline, Ayleen, Eilean, Eilleen, Ilene.*

ELAINE (French) Bright, shining. Derivative of Helen. Variations: *Alayna, Alayne, Allaine, Elaina, Elana, Elane, Elanna, Elayn, Elayne, Eleana, Elena, Eleni Alaina, Ellaina, Ellaine, Ellane, Ellayne.*

ELEANOR (English) Mercy. Derivative of Helen. Variations: *Eleanore, Elenore, Eleonora, Eleonore, Elinor, Ellinor.*

ELECTRA (Greek) Shining one. A mythological figure who had her brother kill their mother and her lover in revenge for their father's murder. Variation: *Elektra.*

ELIANA (Hebrew) God has answered my prayers. Variation: *Eliane*

ELIZABETH (Hebrew) I pledge to God. If you were to add up all the derivatives of Elizabeth, you'd undoubtedly end up with the most popular girls' name in the world by far. Variations: *Alzbeta, Babette, Bess, Bessey, Bessi, Bessie, Bessy, Bet, Beta, Beth, Betina, Betine, Betka, Betsey, Betsi, Betsy, Bett, Betta, Bette, Betti, Bettina, Bettine, Betty, Betuska, Boski, Eilis, Elis, Elisa, Elisabet, Elisabeta, Elisabeth, Elisabetta, Elisabette, Elisaka, Elisauet, Elisaveta, Elise, Eliska, Elissa, Elisueta, Eliza, Elizabetta, Elizabette, Elliza, Elsa, Elsbet, Elsbeth, Elsbietka, Elschen, Else, Elsee, Elsi, Elsie, Elspet, Elspeth, Elyse, Elyssa, Elyza, Elzbieta, Elzunia, Isabel, Isabelita, Liazka, Lib, Libbee, Libbey, Libbi, Libbie, Libby, Libbye, Lieschen, Liese, Liesel, Lis, Lisa, Lisbet, Lisbete, Lisbeth, Lise, Lisenka, Lisettina, Lisveta, Liz, Liza, Lizabeth, Lizanka, Lizbeth, Lizka, Lizzi, Lizzie, Lizzy, Vetta, Yelisaveta, Yelizaueta, Yelizaveta, Ysabel, Zizi, ZsiZsi.*

ELLEN (English) Variation of Helen that has become a full-fledged name in its own right. Variations: *Elan, Elen, Elena, Eleni, Elenyl, Ellan, Ellene, Ellie, Ellon, Ellyn, Elyn, Lene, Wily.*

ELSA (Spanish) Noble. Elsa is a pretty name that has long been popular in Scandinavian as well as Hispanic countries. Variations: *Else, Elsie, Elsy.*

EMILY (English) Industrious. Variations: *Aimil, Amalea, Amalia, Amalie, Amelia, Amelie, Ameline, Amy, Eimile, Em, Ema, Emalee, Emalia, Emelda, Emelene, Emelia, Emelina, Emeline, Emelyn, Emelyne, Emera, Emi, Emie, Emila, Emile, Emilea, Emilia, Emilie, Emilka, Emlynne, Emma, Emmalee, Emmali, Emmaline, Emmalynn, Emele, Emmeline, Emmiline, Emylin, Emylynn, Emlyn.*

EMMA (German) Embracing all. Variations: *Em, Emmi, Emmie, Emmy.*

ERICA (Scandinavian) Leader forever. Feminine version of Eric. Erica is also another name for the heather plant. Variations: *Airica, Airika, Ayrika, Enrica, Enricka, Enrika, Ericka, Erika, Errika, Eyrica.*

ERIN (Gaelic) Nickname for Ireland; also used occasionally as a boy's name; translates to western island. Variations: *Erene, Ereni, Eri, Erina, Erinn, Eryn.*

ESMERELDA (Spanish) Emerald. Variations: *Emerant, Emeraude, Esma, Esmaralda, Esmarelda, Esmiralda, Esmirelda, Ezmeralda.*

ESTELLE (English) Star. Variations: *Essie, Essy, Estee, Estela, Estelita, Estella, Estrelita, Estrella, Estrellita, Stelle.*

EUGENIA (Greek) Well born. Feminine version of Eugene. Variations: *Eugena, Eugenie, Eugina.*

EVANGELINE (Greek) Good news. Variations: *Evangelia, Evangelina, Evangeliste.*

EVELYN (French) Hazelnut. Variations: *Aveline, Eoelene, Eveline, Evelyne, Evelynn, Evelynne, Evlin, Evline, Evlun, Evlynn.*

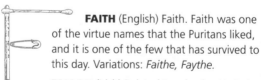

FAITH (English) Faith. Faith was one of the virtue names that the Puritans liked, and it is one of the few that has survived to this day. Variations: *Faithe, Faythe.*

FALLON (Irish) Related to a leader. Variation: *Falon.*

FARRAH (English) Pleasant. Variations: *Fara, Farah, Farra.*

FAWN (French) Young deer. Variations: *Faina, Fanya, Fauan, Faun, Faunia, Fawna, Fawne, Fawnia, Fawnya.*

FAY (French) Fairy. Diminutive of Faith. Variations: *Faye, Fayette.*

FELICIA (Latin) Happy; lucky. Feminine version of Felix. Variations: *Falecia, Falicia, Falicie, Falisha, Falishia, Felice, Feliciana, Felicidad, Felicienne, Felicita, Felicitas, Felicity, Felise, Felita, Feliz, Feliza.*

FEODORA (Russian) Gift from God. Feminine version of Theodore.

FIONA (Irish) Fair, white. Variations: *Fionna, Fionne.*

FINOLA (Irish) White shoulders. Variations: *Effie, Ella, Fenella, Finella, Fionnaghuala, Fionneuala, Fionnghuala, Fionnuala, Fionnula, Fionola, Fynella, Nuala.*

FLANNERY (Irish) Red hair.

FLORA (English) Flower. Flora is one of the more popular names in other countries, including Sweden, Britain, Germany, and Russia. Variations: *Fiora, Fiore, Fiorentina, Fiorenza, Fiori, Fleur, Fleurette, Fleurine, Flo, Flor, Florance, Florann, Floranne, Flore, Florella, Florelle,*

Florence, Florencia, Florentia, Florentyna, Florenze, Floretta, Florette, Flori, Floria, Floriana, Florie, Floriese, Florina, Florinda, Florine, Floris, Florrie, Florry, Floss, Flossey, Flossie.

FRANCES (English) One who is from France. Variations: *Fan, Fancy, Fania, Fannee, Fanney, Fannie, Fanny, Fanya, Fran, Franca, Francee, Franceline, Francena, Francene, Francesca, Francetta, Francette, Francey, Franchesca, Francie, Francina, Francine, Francisca, Francoise, Frank, Frankie, Franni, Frannie, Franzetta, Franziska, Paquita.*

FRANCOISE (French) Frenchman.

FREDA (German) Peaceful. Variations: *Freada, Freddi, Freddie, Freddy, Frederica, Frederique, Freeda, Freida, Frida, Frieda, Fritzi, Fryda.*

GABRIELLE (Hebrew) Heroine of God. Feminine version of Gabriel. Gabrielle has already shown signs of cracking the top 50 list of baby names for girls in the United States; this trend should continue. Variations: *Gabbi, Gabby, Gabi, Gabriela, Gabriell, Gabriella, Gaby.*

GAIA (Greek) Earth. Variations: *Gaioa, Gaya.*

GAIL (Hebrew) My father rejoices. Gail started out as a nickname for Abigail, back in the '40s when traditionally American names started to seem a bit stodgy and old-fashioned. Variations: *Gael, Gaile, Gale, Gayle.*

GENEVIEVE (Celtic) White; Celtic woman. Genevieve has tended to be a continental sophisticated name. Variations: *Genavieve, Geneva, Geneve, Geneveeve, Genivieve, Gennie, Genny, Genovera, Genoveva, Gina, Janeva, Jenevieve.*

GERALDINE (French) One who rules with a spear. Feminine version of Gerald. Variations: *Ceraldina, Deraldene, Geralda, Geraldeen, Geralyn, Geralynne, Geri, Gerianna, Gerianne, Gerilynn, Geroldine, Gerry, Jeraldeen, Jeraldene, Jeraldine, Jeralee, Jere, Jeri, Jerilene, Jerrie, Jerrileen, Jerroldeen, Jerry.*

GERIANNE (American) Gerry + Anne.

GILDA (English) Golden.

GINA (Hebrew) Garden; (Italian) Nickname for names such as Regina and Angelina; (Japanese) Silvery. Variations: *Geena, Gena, Ginat, Ginia.*

GIOVANNA (Italian) God is good. Another feminization of John.

GISELLE (English) Oath; hostage. Giselle also is a picture-perfect name for a ballerina; Giselle is a ballet by Gautier. Variations: *Gelsi, Gelsy, Gisela, Gisele, Gisella, Gizela, Gizella.*

GITA (Hindu) Song. Variations: *Geeta, Geetika, Gitanjau, Gitika.*

GLADYS (Welsh) Lame. Form of Claudia. Variations: *Gwladus, Gwladys.*

GLENNETTE (Scottish) Narrow valley. Feminine version of Glenn.

GLORIA (Latin) Glory. Variations: *Gloree, Glori, Glorie, Glorria, Glory.*

GRACE (Latin) Grace. Grace has been around since the Middle Ages, and it has never really gone out of style. It has been especially popular recently. Variations: *Engracie, Graca, Gracey, Graci, Gracia, Graciana, Gracie, Gracy, Gratia, Grazia, Graziella, Grazielle, Graziosa, Grazyna.*

GWENDOLYN (Welsh) Fair brow. Variations: *Guendolen, Guenna, Gwen, Gwenda, Gwendaline, Gwendia, Gwendolen, Gwendolene, Gwendolin, Gwendoline, Gwendolynn, Gwendolynne, Gwenette, Gwennie, Gwenn, Gwenna, Gwenny.*

GWYNETH (Welsh) Happiness. Both Gwyneth and Gwendolyn are popular now. Variations: *Gwenith, Gwennyth, Gwenyth, Gwynith, Gwynn, Gwynna, Gwynne, Gwynneth.*

HA (Vietnamese) River.

HADLEY (English) Meadow of heather. Variations: *Hadlea, Hadlee, Hadleigh.*

HANNAH (Hebrew) Grace. In the Bible, Hannah was mother of the prophet Samuel. In the United States today, Hannah is white-hot.

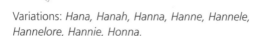

Variations: *Hana, Hanah, Hanna, Hanne, Hannele, Hannelore, Hannie, Honna.*

HARPER (English) Harp player. Harper Lee, author of *To Kill a Mockingbird*, first popularized this traditional last-name-as-first-name for girls.

HARRIET (German) Leader of the house. Feminine version of Harry. Variations: *Harrie, Harrietta, Harriette, Harriot, Harriott, Hatsie, Hatsy, Hattie, Hatty.*

HASIKA (Hindu) Laughter.

HAYLEY (English) Meadow of hay. In the '90s, Hayley became an extremely popular name for girls. Variations: *Hailee, Hailey, Haley, Halie, Halley, Halli, Hallie, Hally, Haylee, Hayleigh, Haylie.*

HEATHER (English) Flower. In this country, Heather has been popular since the '70s.

HEIDI (German) Noble. Variations: *Hedie, Heida, Heide, Heidie, Hydie.*

HELEN (Greek) Light. Helen was a pivotal figure in Greek mythology as the daughter of Zeus, as well as the real-life mother of emperor Constantine the Great back in the fourth century A.D. Variations: *Hela, Hele, Helena, Helene, Hellen, Helli.*

HENRIETTA (German) Leader of the home. Feminine version of Henry. Variations: *Hattie, Hatty, Hendrika, Henka, Hennie, Henrie, Henrieta, Henriette, Henrika, Hetta, Hettie.*

HIALEAH (Native American: Seminole) Beautiful pasture.

HILARY (Greek) Glad. For at least the next few decades, this name will be indelibly connected with Hilary Clinton. Variations: *Hilaria, Hilarie, Hillary, Hillery, Hilliary.*

HISA (Japanese) Everlasting. Many of the more popular names for Japanese girls and boys are meant to impart the hope for longevity to the person with the name. Hisa is one of these names. Variations: *Hisae, Hisako, Hisayo.*

HOLLY (English) Plant. Though Holly has always been more popular in England than in the United States, it should pick up over here in coming years. Variations: *Hollee, Holley, Holli, Hollie, Hollyann.*

HONG (Vietnamese) Pink.

HOSANNA (Greek) Cry of prayer. Variation: *Hosannie*.

HUNTER (English) Hunter.

IDA (English) Youth. Ida was a big name fifty to one hundred years ago, which brought forth the Gilbert and Sullivan opera *Princess Ida*. Variations: *Idalene, Idalia, Idalina, Idaline, Idalya, Idalyne, Ide, Idell, Idella, Idelle, Idetta, Idette, Idia*.

IMELDA (Italian) Embracing the fight. Variation: *Imalda*.

INDIA (English) The country.

INDIGO (Latin) Dark blue.

INGA (Scandinavian) In Norse mythology, god of fertility and peace. Variations: *Ingaar, Inge, Ingo, Ingvio*.

INGRID (Scandinavian) Beautiful.

IRENE (Greek) Peace. Irene has a long and rich history. One Irene became a saint in the fourth century A.D. Even before that, Irene was one of the more popular names during the Roman Empire. Variations: *Arina*,

Arinka, Eirena, Eirene, Eirini, Erena, Erene, Ereni, Errena, Irayna, Ireen, Iren, Irena, Irenea, Irenee, Irenka, Irina, Irine, Irini, Irisha, Irka, Irusya, Iryna, Orina, Orya, Oryna, Reena, Reenie, Rina, Yarina, Yaryna.

ISABEL (Spanish) Pledge of God. Version of Elizabeth. Variations: *Isa, Isabeau, Isabelita, Isabella, Isabelle, Isobel, Issi, Issie, Issy, Izabel, Izabele, Izabella, Izabelle, Izebela, Ysabel.*

ISADORA (Latin) Gift from Isis. Feminine version of Isidore. Variation: *Isidora.*

ISMAELA (Hebrew) God listens. Variations: *Isma, Mael, Maella.*

ITALIA (Latin) From Italy. Variation: *Talia.*

ITO (Japanese) Fiber.

IVANA (Slavic) God is good. Feminine version of Ivan. Variations: *Iva, Ivania, Ivanka, Ivanna, Ivannia.*

IVORY (Latin) Ivory. Variations: *Ivoreen, Ivorine.*

IVY (English) Plant. Variations: *Iva, Ivey, Ivie.*

JACEY (American) Newly created, possibly from the letters "J" and "C." Variations: *Jace, Jacy.*

JACINTA (Spanish) Hyacinth. Feminine version of Jacinto. Variations: *Glacinda, Glacintha, Jacinda, Jacintha, Jacinthe, Jacinthia, Jacki, Jacky, Jacquetta, Jacqui, Jacquie, Jacynth, Jacyntha, Jacynthe.*

JACQUELINE (French) He who replaces. Feminine version of Jacob. Variations: *Jacaline, Jacalyn, Jackalin, Jackalyn, Jackeline, Jackelyn, Jacketta, Jackette, Jacki, Jackie, Jacklin, Jacklyn, Jacky, Jaclyn, Jaclynn, Jacoba, Jacobette, Jacobina, Jacolyn, Jacqualine, Jacqualyn, Jacqualynn, Jacquelean, Jacquelene, Jacquelin, Jacquelyn, Jacquelyne, Jacquelynn, Jacquelynne, Jacqueta, Jacquetta, Jacquiline, Jacquline, Jacqulynn, Jaculine, Jakelyn, Jaqueline, Jaquelyn, Jaquith.*

JADE (Spanish) Jade stone. Variations: *Jada, Jadee, Jadira, Jady, Jaida, Jaide, Jayde, Jaydra.*

JAIMIE (English) One who replaces. Feminine version of James. Variations: *Jaime, Jaimey, Jaimi, Jaimy, Jamee, Jami, Jamie, Jayme*.

JANINE (English) God is good. Feminine version of John. Variations: *Janina, Jannine, Jeneen, Jenine*.

JASMINE (Persian) Flower. Variations: *Jasmeen, Jasmin, Jasmina, Jazmin, Jazmine, Jessamine, Jessamyn, Yasiman, Yasman, Yasmine*.

JAYNE (Hindu) Victorious.

JENNA (Arabic) Little bird. Variations: *Jannarae, Jena, Jenesi, Jenn, Jennabel, Jennah, Jennalee, Jennalyn, Jennasee*.

JENNIFER (Welsh) White; smooth; soft. Jennifer is a version of Guinevere. It is perhaps the best example of the kind of trendy names that exploded in popularity overnight in the mid-'70s all the way up to the early '90s before almost completely burning out. Although it is still used today, it was so popular that many parents might tend to shy away from using it today. Variations: *Genn, Gennifer, Genny, Ginnifer, Jen, Jena, Jenalee, Jenalyn, Jenarae, Jenene, Jenetta Jenita, Jennis, Jeni, Jenice,*

Jeniece, Jenifer, Jeniffer, Jenilee, Jenilynn, Jenise, Jenn, Jennessa, Jenni, Jennie, Jennika, Jennilyn, Jennyann, Jennylee, Jeny, Jinny.

JERALYN (American) Combination of Jerry and Marilyn. Variations: *Jerelyn, Jerilyn, Jerilynn, Jerralyn, Jerrilyn.*

JESSICA (Hebrew) He sees. Like Jennifer, Jessica was a regular fixture on the baby name hit parade from the mid-'70s all the way through to the late '80s. It made its first appearance in the Bible in the book of Genesis. Parents today are choosing other variations related to Jessica. Variations: *Jesica, Jess, Jessa, Jesse, Jesseca, Jessey, Jessi, Jessie, Jessika.*

JILL (English) Young. Shortened version of Juliana. Variations: *Gil, Gill, Gyl, Gyll, Jil, Jilli, Jillie, Jilly, Jyl, Jyll.*

JOANNE (English) God is good. Variations: *Joana, Joanna, Joannah, Johanna, Johanne.*

JOCELYN (English) Unknown definition, possibly a combination of Joyce and Lynn. Variations: *Jocelin,*

Joceline, Jocelyne, Joci, Jocie, Josaline, Joscelin, Josceline, Joscelyn, Joseline, Joselyn, Joselyne, Josiline, Josline.

JOELLE (French) God is Lord. Feminine version of Joel. Variations: *Joda, Joell, Joella, Joellen, Joellyn, Joely.*

JOLENE (American) Jolene is a combination name, formed by using "Jo" and "lene." Jolene is considered by some to be a contemporary version of Josephine. Variations: *Jolean, Joleen, Jolian, Jolin, Joline, Jolinn, Jolinne, Jolyn, Jolynn, Jolynne, Jolyon.*

JOLIE (French) Pretty. *Variations: Jolee, Joley, Joli, Joline, Joly.*

JORDAN (English) To descend. During the Crusades, Christians who returned home brought water from the Jordan river for the express purpose of baptizing their children. Many of those children were named Jordan— the boys at least. Variations: *Jordana, Jordon, Jordyn.*

JOSEPHINE (Hebrew) God will add. Feminine version of Joseph. Variations: *Jo, Joey, Jojo, Josefa, Josefina, Josefine, Josepha, Josephe, Josephene, Josephina, Josetta, Josette, Josey, Josi, Josie.*

JOYCE (Latin) Joyous. Joyce started out as a boys' name. It was the name of a saint in the seventh century A.D. This usage continued occasionally until the late Middle Ages, but Joyce started to be regularly used only during the nineteenth century. Variations: *Jitka, Jucika, Judey, Judi, Judie, Judit, Judita, Judite, Juditha, Judithe, Judy, Judye, Jutka.*

JULIA (English) Young. Roman clan name. Julia is popular all over the world and has been since women in ancient Rome gave the name to their babies in honor of the emperor Julius Caesar. Variations: *Iulia, Jula, Julcia, Julee, Juley, Juli, Juliana, Juliane, Julianna, Julianne, Julica, Julie, Julina, Juline, Julinka, Juliska, Julissa, Julka, Yula, Yulinka, Yuliya, Yulka, Yulya.*

JYOTI (Hindu) Light of the moon. Variation: *Jyotsana.*

KAI (Japanese) Forgiveness; (Hawaiian) Sea. Kai frequently occurs in many Hawaiian place names. Kai has just recently started to appear in the United States as a name for girls. Variations: *Kaiko, Kaiyo*.

KAITLIN (English) Combination of Kate and Lynn. Variations: *Kaitlinn, Kaitlinne, Kaitlynn, Katelin, Katelyn, Katelynne*.

KALLI (Greek) Singing lark. Variations: *Cal, Calli, Callie, Colli, Kal, Kallie, Kallu, Kally*.

KAMELIA (Hawaiian) Vineyard. Variation: *Komela*.

KARA (Latin) Dear. Variations: *Kaira, Karah, Karalee, Karalyn, Karalynn, Kari, Kariana, Karianna, Karianne, Karie, Karielle, Karrah, Karrie, Kary*.

KAREN (Scandinavian) Diminutive of Katerina. Variations: *Caren, Carin, Caryn, Karin, Karina, Karon, Kerena*.

KATHERINE (Greek) Pure. Katherine and all of its derivatives have been popular since the days of its Greek origin, when it was known as Aikaterina. Variations: *Caitriona, Caren, Caron, Caryn, Caye, Kaethe, Kai, Kaila, Kait, Kaitlin,*

Karen, Karena, Karin, Karina, Karine, Karon, Karyn, Karyna, Karynn, Kata, Kataleen, Katalin, Katalina, Katarina, Kate, Katee, Kateke, Katerina, Katerinka, Katey, Katharin, Katharina, Katharine, Katharyn, Kathereen, Katherin, Katherina, Kathey, Kathi, Kathie, Kathleen, Kathlyn, Kathlynn, Kathren, Kathrine, Kathryn, Kathryne, Kathy, Kati, Katia, Katica, Katie, Katina, Katrina, Katrine, Katriona, Katryna, Kattrina, Katushka, Katy, Karrin, Katya, Kay, Kisan, Kit, Kitti, Kittie, Kitty, Kotinka, Kotryna, Yekaterina.

KAYLA (English) Pure. Variation of Katherine. Kayla may have started to become popular about the same time that the name Caleb started to appear more frequently for boys. Variations: *Kaela, Kaelee, Kaelene, Kaeli, Kaeleigh, Kaelie, Kaelin, Kaelyn, Kaila, Kailan, Kailee, Kaileen, Kailene, Kailey, Kailin, Kailynne, Kalan, Kalee, Kaleigh, Kalen, Kaley, Kalie, Kalin, Kalyn, Kayana, Kayanna, Kaye, Kaylan, Kaylea, Kayleen, Kayleigh, Kaylene, Kayley, Kayli, Kaylle.*

KAYA (Native American) Wise child.

KEESHA (African-American) Newly created. Variations: *Keisha, Keshia, Kiesha.*

KELLY (Irish) Female soldier. Kelly was at its most popular in the '70s, and parents who have selected the name for their daughter since then have often selected one of the name's variations. Variations: *Kealey, Kealy, Keeley, Keelie, Keellie, Keely, Keighley, Keiley, Keilly, Keily, Kellee, Kelley, Kellia, Kellie, Kellina, Kellisa.*

KELSEY (English) Island. Kelsey captivated many parents-to-be during the mid-to-late '80s, as a name for girls. Variations: *Kelcey, Kelci, Kelcie, Kelcy, Kellsie, Kelsa, Kelsea, Kelsee, Kelseigh, Kelsi, Kelsie, Kelsy.*

KENDRA (English) Origin unknown; possibly a combination of Kenneth and Sandra. Variations: *Kena, Kenadrea, Kendria, Kenna, Kindra, Kinna, Kyndra.*

KENISHA (African-American) Beautiful woman. Variations: *Keneisha, Keneshia, Kennesha.*

KERRY (Irish) County in Ireland. Like its counter-part Kelly, Kerry started out as a boys' name. Variations: *Kera, Keree, Keri, Keriana, Keriann, Kerianna, Kerianne, Kerra, Kerrey, Kerri, Kerrianne, Kerrie.*

KESIA (African-American) Favorite. Variation: *Keshia.*

KIMBERLY (English) King's meadow. Kimberly was one of the most popular names in the '60s and '70s. Today, however, it appears less frequently both here and in Britain. Variations: *Kim, Kimba, Kimba Lee, Kimball, Kimber, Kimberlea, Kimberlee, Kimberlei, Kimberleigh, Kimberley, Kimberli, Kimberlie, Kimberlyn, Kimbley, Kimmi, Kimmie, Kymberlee.*

KIRA (Bulgarian) Throne. Variations: *Kiran, Kirana, Kiri, Kirra.*

KIRSTEN (Scandinavian) Anointed. Feminine version of Christian. Variations: *Keerstin, Kersten, Kersti, Kerstie, Kerstin, Kiersten, Kierstin, Kirsta, Kirsti, Kirstie, Kirstin, Kirstine, Kirsty, Kirstyn, Kirstynn, Kyrstin.*

KITRA (Hebrew) Wreath.

KOKO (Japanese) Stork.

KRISTEN (English) Anointed. Feminine version of Christian. Kristen has only been around in any measure since the '60s in the United States. Kristen is one of the more popular girls' names around these days, but is not yet overused. Variations: *Krista, Kristan, Kristin, Kristina, Kristine, Kristyn, Kristyna, Krysta, Krystyna.*

KYLE (Scottish) Narrow land. This highly popular '90s name for boys has already started to develop a following among girls.

KYOKO (Japanese) Mirror.

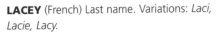

LACEY (French) Last name. Variations: *Laci, Lacie, Lacy.*

LADONNA (African-American) Newly created. Variations: *Ladon, Ladonne, Ladonya.*

LAINE (English) Bright one. Variation of Helen. Variations: *Lainey, Lane, Layne.*

LAKEISHA (African-American) Newly created. Variations: *Lakecia, Lakeesha, Lakesha, Lakeshia, Laketia, Lakeysha, Lakeyshia, Lakicia, Lakiesha, Lakisha, Lakitia, Laquiesha, Laquiesha, Laquisha, Lekeesha, Lekeisha, Lekisha.*

LARISSA (Greek) Happy. Variations: *Laresa, Laressa, Larisa, Laryssa.*

LASHANDA (African-American) Newly created.

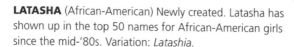

LATASHA (African-American) Newly created. Latasha has shown up in the top 50 names for African-American girls since the mid-'80s. Variation: *Latashia*.

LATOYA (African-American) Newly created. Variations: *Latoia, Latoyia, Latoyla*.

LAURA (Latin) Laurel. Laura has appeared in the top 25 list of girls' names since the mid-'70s. Laura has been equally popular both in the United States and in Britain. Variations: *Larette, Laural, Laure, Laureana, Laurel, Lauren, Laurena, Lauret, Laureta, Lauretta, Laurette, Laurie, Laurin, Lauryn, Lora, Loren, Lorena, Loret, Loreta, Loretta, Lorette, Lori, Lorin, Lorita, Lorrie, Lorrin, Lorry, Loryn*.

LEAH (Hebrew) Weary. Leah, in the book of Genesis, was first used as a given name in sixteenth-century Puritan England. Variations: *Lea, Leia, Leigha, Lia, Liah*.

LEANNA (Gaelic) Flowering vine. Variations: *Leana, Leane, Leann, Leanne, Lee Ann, Lee Anne, Leeann, Leeanne, Leianna, Leigh Ann, Leighann, Leighanne, Liana, Liane, Lianne*.

LEIGH (English) Meadow. Variation: *Lee*.

LEIKO (Japanese) Proud.

LENA (English) Bright one. Variation of Helen. Variations: *Lenah, Lene, Leni, Lenia, Lina, Linah, Line.*

LESLIE (Scottish) Low meadow. Variations: *Leslea, Leslee, Lesley, Lesli, Lesly, Lezlee, Lezley, Lezli, Lezlie.*

LILITH (Arabic) Night demon. Lilith is the wife that Adam had before Eve. According to legend, Lilith didn't like having a man calling the shots, so she departed, turning herself into a demon instead. Variation: *Lillis.*

LILLIAN (English) Lily + Ann. Variations: *Lileana, Lilian, Liliana, Lilias, Lilika, Lillia, Lillianne, Lillyan, Lillyanna, Lilyan.*

LILY (Latin) Flower. Variations: *Lili, Lilia, Lilie, Lilli, Lillie, Lillye, Lilye.*

LINDSAY (English) Island of linden trees. Variations: *Lindsaye, Lindsey, Lindsi, Lindsie, Lindsy, Linsay, Linsey, Linzey, Lyndsay, Lyndsey, Lynsay, Lynsey.*

LINETTE (Welsh) Idol. Variations: *Lanette, Linet, Linetta, Linnet, Linnetta, Linnette, Lynetta, Lynette, Lynnet, Lynnette.*

LISA (English) Pledged by oath to God. Version of Elizabeth. Variations: *Leesa, Leeza, Leisa, Liesa, Liese, Lisanne, Lise, Liseta, Lisetta, Lisette, Lissa, Lissette, Liza, Lizana, Lizanne, Lizette.*

LISANDRA (Greek) Liberator. Variations: *Lissandra, Lizandra, Lizann, Lizanne, Lysandra.*

LOLA (English) Sorrow. Nickname for Dolores. Variations: *Loleta, Loletta, Lolita.*

LORELEI (German) Area in Germany. Variations: *Loralee, Loralie, Loralyn, Lorilee, Lura, Lurette, Lurleen, Lurlene, Lurline.*

LORRAINE (French) Area in France. Variations: *Laraine, Lauraine, Laurraine, Lorain, Loraine, Lorayne, Lorine, Lorrayne.*

LOUISE (English) Famous soldier. Feminine version of Louis. Variations: *Aloise, Aloysia, Louisine, Louiza, Luisa, Luise.*

LUCY (English) Light. Feminine version of Lucius. Lucia, the root for all Lucy-related names, is in turn the feminine version of an ancient Roman family name. Today, parents are choosing Lucy more often. Variations: *Lucetta, Lucette, Lucia, Luciana, Lucie, Lucienne, Lucilla, Lucille, Lucina, Lucinda, Lucita.*

LYDIA (Greek) Woman from Lydia, a region in ancient Greece. Variations: *Lidi, Lidia, Lidie, Lidka, Likochka, Lydiah, Lydie.*

MABEL (English) Lovable. Variations: *Mabelle, Mable, Maybel, Maybell, Maybelle.*

MADELINE (French) Mary Magdalen. Most parents today are familiar with the Madeleine books by the author Ludwig Bemelmans. Variations: *Mada, Madalaina, Maddalena, Maddi, Maddie, Madelaine, Madelayne, Madeleine, Madelena, Madelene, Madelina, Madge, Magda.*

MADISON (English) Last name.

MALLORY (French) Unfortunate. Variations: *Malloreigh, Mallorey, Mallorie, Malorey, Malori, Malorie, Malory.*

MARCIA (Latin) Warlike. Feminine version of Mark. Variations: *Marce, Marcee, Marcela, Marcelia, Marcella, Marcelle, Marcena, Marcene, Marcey, Marci, Marcie, Marcina, Marcy, Marsha.*

MARGARET (English) Pearl. Variations: *Greeta, Greetje, Grere, Gret, Greta, Gretal, Gretchen, Gretel, Grethal, Grethel, Gretje, Gretl, Gretta, Groer, Maggi, Maggie, Maggy, Mair, Maire, Mairi, Mairona, Margara, Margareta, Margarethe, Margarett, Margaretta, Margarette, Margarita, Margarite, Marge, Margeret, Margerey, Margery, Margrett, Marguerette, Marguerite, Marj, Marjorie, Meagan, Meaghan, Meaghen, Meg, Megan, Megen, Meggi, Meggie, Meggy, Meghan, Meghann, Peg, Pegeen, Pegg, Peggey, Peggi, Peggie, Peggy, Reet, Reeta, Reita, Rheeta, Riet, Rieta, Ritta.*

MARIE (French) Variation of Mary. Today in the United States, Marie is still used more frequently than Mary and Maria combined.

MARILYN (English) Combination of Mary and Lynn. Variations: *Maralin, Maralynn, Marelyn, Marilee, Marilin, Marilynne, Marralynn, Marrilin, Marrilyn, Marylin, Marylyn.*

MARIS (Latin) Star of the sea. Variations: *Marieca, Marisa, Marise, Marish, Marisha, Marissa, Marisse, Meris, Merisa, Merissa.*

MARLENE (English) Combination of Maria and Magdalene. Variations: *Marla, Marlaina, Marlaine, Marlana, Marlane, Marlayne, Marlea, Marlee, Marleen, Marleina, Marlena, Marley, Marlie, Marlina, Marlinda, Marline, Marlyn.*

MARY (Hebrew) Bitterness. The Virgin Mary. Back in the Middle Ages, you could be tried for blasphemy if you chose the name Mary for your

daughter; back then, it was considered to be too sacred to use for a mere mortal. Of course, once attitudes changed, Mary quickly grew to become one of the most popular names among English-speaking countries. Variations: *Maree, Marella, Marelle, Mari, Marial, Marieke, Mariel, Mariela, Mariele, Mariella, Marielle, Marika, Marike, Maryk, Maura, Moira, Moll, Mollee, Molley, Molli, Mollie, Molly, Mora, Moria, Moyra.*

MATILDA (Old German) Maiden in battle. Variations: *Maddi, Maddie, Maddy, Mat, Matelda, Mathilda, Mathilde, Matilde, Mattie, Matty, Matusha, Matylda, Maud, Maude, Tila, Tilda, Tildie, Tildy, Tilley, Tilli, Tillie, Tilly, Tylda.*

MAUREEN (Irish) Variation of Mary. Maureen was a quintessentially Irish name that appeared to be equally popular in Ireland, Britain, and the United States in the mid-twentieth century. Then it began to become used less frequently. Variations: *Maurene, Maurine, Moreen, Morreen, Moureen.*

MELANIE (Greek) Dark-skinned. Variations: *Mel, Mela, Melaine, Melana, Melane, Melani, Melaniya, Melanka, Melany, Melanya, Melashka, Melasya, Melenia, Melka,*

Mellanie, Mellie, Melloney, Mellony, Melly, Meloni, Melonie, Melony, Milena, Milya.

MELINDA (Latin) Honey. Variations: *Malina, Malinda, Malinde, Mallie, Mally, Mel, Meleana, Melina, Melinde, Meline, Mellinda, Melynda, Mindi, Mindie, Mindy.*

MELISSA (Greek) Bee. Melissa is an ancient name that was first popular during the early Roman Empire as it was the name of the woman who nursed the mighty god Juno when he was a baby. Variations: *Melisa, Melisande, Melisandra, Melisandre, Melissande, Melissandre, Melisse, Mellisa, Mellissa.*

MENASHA (Native American: Algonquin) Island.

MERCEDES (Spanish) Mercy. Variations: *Merced, Mercede.*

MEREDITH (Welsh) Great leader. Variations: *Meredithe, Merideth, Meridith, Merridith.*

MERYL (English) Bright as the sea. Variations: *Merill, Merrall, Merrel, Merrell, Merrill, Meryle, Meryll.*

MICHAELA (Hebrew) Who is like the Lord? Feminine version of Michael. Variations: *Makaela, Micaela, Mical,*

Michael, Michaella, Michal, Michala, Mickaula, Micki, Mickie, Micky, Mikella, Mikelle, Mychaela.

MICHELLE (French) Who is like the Lord? More common feminine version of Michael. Michelle has been one of the few names that has been in the top 10 list since the '60s. Variations: *Michele, Nichelle.*

MIDORI (Japanese) Green.

MING (Chinese) Tomorrow.

MIRABEL (Latin) Wonderful. Variations: *Mirabell, Mirabella, Mirabelle.*

MIRANDA (Latin) Admirable. Variations: *Maranda, Meranda, Mira, Myranda, Randa, Randee, Randene, Randey, Randi, Randie, Randy.*

MIYO (Japanese) Beautiful generations. Variation: *Miyoko.*

MONICA (Latin) Adviser or nun. Variations: *Monika, Monique.*

MORGAN (Welsh) Great and bright. Variations: *Morgana, Morganne, Morgen.*

MURIEL (Irish) Bright as the sea. Variations: *Muirgheal, Murial, Muriell, Murielle.*

MYRA (Latin) Scented oil. Feminine version of Myron. Variations: *Murah, Myria, Myriah.*

NADA (Arabic) Dew at sunrise. Variation: *Nadya.*

NADIA (Russian) Hope. Variations: *Nada, Nadeen, Nadene, Nadina, Nadine, Nadiya, Nadja, Nadya, Natka.*

NANCY (Hebrew) Grace. Though its origins are Hebrew, Nancy seems more like one of the quintessentially American names. Nancy's peak in the United States occurred in the '50s, when it placed in the top ten. Variations: *Nan, Nana, Nance, Nancee, Nancey, Nanci, Nancie, Nancsi, Nanette, Nann, Nanna, Nanncey, Nanncy, Nanni, Nannie, Nanny, Nanscey, Nansee, Nansey.*

NAOMI (Hebrew) Pleasant. Variations: *Naoma, Naomia, Naomie, Neoma, Noami, Noemi, Noemie.*

NATALIE (Latin) Birthday. Variations: *Natala, Natalee, Natalene, Natalia, Natalina, Nataline, Natalka, Natalya, Natelie, Nathalia, Nathalie.*

NATASHA (Greek) Rebirth. Variations: *Nastasia, Nastassia, Nastassja, Nastassya, Nastasya, Natashia, Tashi, Tashia, Tasis, Tassa, Tassie.*

NELL (English) Light. Back around the turn of the century, when the name was first popular, the variation Nellie was more common than its root. Today, both should grow in popularity as both a first and middle name. Variations: *Nella, Nelley, Nelli, Nellie, Nelly.*

NEVADA (English) The state.

NICOLE (English) People of victory. Feminine version of Nicholas. Variations: *Nichol, Nichola, Nichole, Nicholle, Nicki, Nickola, Nickole, Nicola, Nicoleen, Nicolene, Nicoletta, Nicolette, Nicolina, Nicoline, Nicolla, Nicolle, Nikki, Nikola, Nikoletta, Nikolette.*

NINA (Spanish) Girl. In Babylonian mythology, Nina was the goddess of the seas, and in the Incan culture, Nina ruled over fire. In this country, it seems as if Nina may well start to become more visible. Variations: *Neena, Ninelle, Ninet, Nineta, Ninete, Ninetta, Ninette, Ninita, Ninnette, Ninotchka, Nynette.*

NITA (Hindu) Friendly. Variations: *Neeta, Nitali.*

NOEL (French) Christmas. The variation Nowell appears to have come about because this is how the holiday is spelled in many Christmas carols. Variations: *Noela, Noelani, Noele, Noeleen, Noelene, Noeline, Noell, Noella, Noelle, Noelline, Noleen, Nowell.*

NOLA (English) White shoulder. Variations: *Nolah, Nolana.*

NORA (Greek) Light. Variation: *Norah.*

NOREEN (English) Diminutive of Nora, light. Variations: *Noreena, Norene, Norina, Norine.*

NORMA (Latin) Pattern. Variation: *Normah.*

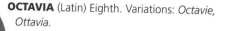

OCTAVIA (Latin) Eighth. Variations: *Octavie, Ottavia.*

ODE (African: Nigerian) Born while traveling.

ODELE (German) Wealthy. Variations: *Oda, Odeela, Odela, Odelia, Odelinda, Odell, Odella, Odelle, Odelyn, Odila, Odile, Odilia.*

ODETTE (French) Wealthy. Variation: *Odetta.*

OLA (Polish) Protector of men; (Scandinavian) Ancestor's relic. Variations: *Olesia, Olesya.*

OLGA (Russian) Holy. Olga is one of the more popular names in Russia today, but it is also widely used across Europe. Variations: *Elga, Ola, Olenka, Olesya, Olia, Olina, Olka, Olli, Olly, Olunka, Oluska, Olva, Olya, Olyusha.*

OLIVIA (Latin) Olive tree. Though its roots are Italian, most Americans tend to think of Olivia as a very British name. Olivia made its first appearance in literature in Shakespeare's play *Twelfth Night.* Variations: *Lioa, Lioia, Liovie, Liv, Olia, Oliva, Olive, Olivet, Olivette, Olivine, Ollie, Olva.*

OPAL (English) Gem. Variations: *Opalina, Opaline.*

OPHELIA (Greek) Help. Variation: *Ofelia*.

ORIANA (Latin) Sunrise. Variations: *Oraine, Oralia, Orane, Orania, Orelda, Orelle, Oriane*.

PAGE (French) Intern. Variation: *Paige*.

PAMELA (Greek) Honey. The name Pamela first appeared in a popular novel entitled *Pamela* by Samuel Richardson, in the middle of the eighteenth century. Variations: *Pam, Pamala, Pamalia, Pamalla, Pamelia, Pamelina, Pamella, Pamilia, Pamilla, Pammela, Pammi, Pammie, Pammy*.

PARIS (English) The city. Variations: *Parisa, Parris, Parrish*.

PASCALE (French) Child of Easter. Feminine version of Pascal. Variations: *Pascalette, Pascaline, Pascalle, Paschale*.

PATRICIA (English) Noble. Feminine version of Patrick. Patricia has a long, esteemed history dating from the sixth century. A surge in its popularity can clearly be distinguished from the time that one of Queen Victoria's granddaughters was given the name. From there, it basically exploded in both Great Britain and the United States. Variations: *Pat, Patreece, Patreice, Patria, Patric, Patrica, Patrice, Patricka, Patrizia, Patsy, Patti, Pattie, Patty, Tricia, Trish, Trisha.*

PAULA (Latin) Small. Feminine version of Paul. Variations: *Paola, Paolina, Paule, Pauleen, Paulene, Pauletta, Paulette, Paulie, Paulina, Pauline, Paulita, Pauly, Paulyn, Pavla, Pavlina, Pavlinka, Pawlina, Pola, Polcia, Pollie, Polly.*

PEARL (Latin) Pearl. Variations: *Pearla, Pearle, Pearleen, Pearlena, Pearlette, Pearley, Pearline, Pearly, Perl, Perla, Perle, Perlette, Perley, Perlie, Perly.*

PENELOPE (Greek) Bobbin weaver. Penelope is a great worldly name that dates back to the ancient Greek myth in which Penelope remained faithful to Ulysses. Variations: *Lopa, Pela, Pelcia, Pen, Penelopa, Penina, Penine, Penna, Pennelope, Penni, Penny, Pinelopi, Piptisa, Popi.*

PERRY (French) Pear tree; (Greek) Nymph of mountains. Perry started out as a boys' name that was actually a nickname for Peregrine. Variations: *Peri, Perrey, Perri, Perrie.*

PHILIPPA (Greek) Lover of horses. Feminine version of Philip. Variations: *Philipa, Philippine, Phillipina, Pippa, Pippy.*

PHYLLIS (Greek) Green tree branch. Variations: *Philis, Phillis, Philliss, Phyllys, Phylis, Phyllida, Phylliss.*

PIA (Latin) Pious.

POLLY (English) Variation of Molly, which in turn is a diminutive form of Mary, which means bitter. Variations: *Pauleigh, Pollee, Polley, Polli, Pollie, Pollyann, Pollyanna, Pollyanne.*

PORTIA (Latin) Roman clan name. Variations: *Porcha, Porscha, Porsche, Porschia, Porsha.*

PRISCILLA (English) Old. Priscilla was a popular Puritan name. Today, however, the widow of Elvis Presley, Priscilla Presley, has altered its reputation from prim and proper to smart and alluring. Variations: *Precilla, Prescilla, Pricilla, Pris, Priscila, Priss, Prissie, Prissilla, Prissy, Prysilla.*

QUINN (Gaelic) Advisor. Variation: *Quincy.*

RACHEL (Hebrew) Lamb. Rachel is essentially one of the oldest names in the Bible. In the '90s, Rachel consistently appeared in the top 20 names list. Variations: *Rachael, Racheal, Rachele, Rachell, Rachelle, Rae, Raelene, Raquel, Raquela, Raquella, Raquelle.*

RAFAELA (Spanish) God heals. Feminine version of Raphael. Variations: *Rafa, Rafaelia, Rafaella, Rafella, Rafelle, Raffaela, Raffaele, Raphaella, Raphaelle, Refaela, Rephaela.*

RAMONA (Hindu) Wise protector. Feminine version of Raymond. Many parents casting around for a suitable name for their daughters will remember Ramona primarily as the impish character in the children's books by author Beverly Cleary.

RASHEDA (Turkish) Righteous. Feminine version of Rashid. Variations: *Rasheeda, Rasheedah, Rasheida, Rashidah.*

RAYNA (Hebrew) Song of the Lord. Variations: *Raina, Rana, Rane, Rania, Renana, Renanit, Renatia, Renatya, Renina, Rinatia, Rinatya.*

REBECCA (Hebrew) Joined together. The first Rebecca known to us was the Biblical wife of Isaac and the mother of Jacob. Variations: *Becca, Becky, Reba, Rebbecca, Rebbie, Rebeca, Rebeccah, Rebecka, Rebeckah, Rebeka, Rebekah, Rebekka, Rebekke, Rebeque, Rebi, Reby, Reyba, Rheba.*

RENÉE (French) Reborn. The Latin version of Renée is Renata, and it was commonly used by people in the Roman Empire for their daughters. Variations: *Renata, Renay, Rene, Renelle, Reney, Reni, Renia, Renie, Renni, Rennie, Renny.*

RHIANNON (Welsh) Goddess. Variations: *Rheanna, Rheanne, Rhiana, Rhiann, Rhianna, Rhiannan, Rhianon, Rhuan, Riana, Riane, Rianna, Rianne, Riannon, Riannon, Rianon, Riona.*

ROBERTA (English) Bright fame. Feminine version of Robert. Variations: *Bobbet, Bobbett, Bobbi, Bobbie, Bobby, Robbi, Robbie, Robby, Robena, Robertena,*

Robertha, Robertina, Robin, Robina, Robine, Robinette, Robinia, Robyn, Robyna, Rogan, Roynne.

ROCHELLE (French) Little rock. Variations: Rochele, Rochell, Rochella, Roshele, Roshelle.

ROLANDA (German) Famous land. Feminine version of Roland. Variations: Rolande, Rollande, Rolonda, Rolonde.

ROSALIND (Spanish) Pretty rose. Variations: Rosalina, Rosalinda, Rosalinde, Rosaline, Rosalyn, Rosalynd, Rosalyne, Rosalynn, Roselind, Roselynn, Roslyn.

ROSANNA (English) Combination of Rose and Anna. Variations: Rosana, Rosannah, Rosanne, Roseana, Roseanna, Roseanna, Roseannah, Rosehannah, Rozanna, Rozanne.

ROSE (Latin) Flower. Variations: Rosabel, Rosabell, Rosabella, Rosabelle, Rosalee, Rosaley, Rosalia, Rosalie, Rosalin, Rosella, Roselle, Rosetta, Rosette, Rosey, Rosi, Rosie, Rosita, Rosy, Ruza, Ruzena, Ruzenka, Ruzsa.

ROSEMARY (Latin) Dew of the sea. Variations: *Rosemaree, Rosemarey, Rosemaria, Rosemarie.*

ROSSALYN (Scottish) Cape. Feminine version of Ross. Variations: *Rosslyn, Rosslynn.*

ROXANNE (Persian) Dawn. Variations: *Roxana, Roxane, Roxann, Roxanna, Roxianne, Roxie, Roxy.*

RUBY (English) Jewel. Variations: *Rube, Rubey, Rubie, Rubye.*

RUTH (Hebrew) Companion. Variations: *Ruthe, Ruthella, Ruthelle, Ruthetta, Ruthi, Ruthie, Ruthina, Ruthine, Ruthy.*

SACHI (Japanese) Bliss. Variation: *Sachiko.*

SAMANTHA (English) His name is God. Samantha is widely considered to be the feminine version of Samuel, and though it's been around from the 1600s, it's still a popular girls' name today. Variations: *Sam, Samella, Samentha, Sammantha, Sammee, Sammey, Sammi,*

Sammie, Sammy, Semanntha, Semantha, Simantha, Symantha.

SARAH (Hebrew) Princess. In the Bible, Sarah was the wife of Abraham, and the name has been well-used and well-liked in both Great Baritain and the United States since Puritan times. Variations: *Sadee, Sadie, Sadye, Saidee, Saleena, Salena, Salina, Sallee, Salley, Sallianne, Sallie, Sally, Sallyann, Sara, Sarai, Saretta, Sarette, Sari, Sarita, Saritia, Sarra.*

SAVANNAH (Spanish) Treeless. Place name. Variations: *Savana, Savanah, Savanna, Savonna, Sevanna.*

SCARLETT (English) Red. Variations: *Scarlet, Scarlette.*

SELA (Polynesian) Princess.

SELENA (Greek) Goddess of the moon. Though Selena's first use was as a Greek goddess, the name began to become popular in the 1800s when a countess in Britain went by the name of Selina. Variations: *Celena, Celina, Celinda, Celine, Celyna, Salena, Salina, Salinah, Sela, Selene, Selina, Selinda, Seline, Sena.*

SERENA (Latin) Serene. Variations: *Sareen, Sarena, Sarene, Sarina, Sarine, Sereena, Serenah, Serenna, Serina.*

SHALONDA (African-American) Newly created.

SHANIKA (African-American) Newly created. Variations: *Shaneeka, Shaneeke, Shanicka, Shanikah, Shaniqua, Shanique, Shenika.*

SHANNON (Irish) Ancient. Shannon first appeared as a girls' name in the United States, back in the '30s. Britain had only started to discover the name by 1950. Bucking the tide, many parents then began to use it for their sons, but the female habit of totally assimilating a boys' name has taken over, and today Shannon is mostly thought of as a girls' name. Variations: *Shanan, Shann, Shanna, Shannah, Shannan, Shannen, Shannie, Shanon.*

SHARMAINE (English) Roman clan name. Variations: *Sharma, Sharmain, Sharman, Sharmane, Sharmayne, Sharmian, Sharmine, Sharmyn.*

SHAYLEEN (African-American) Unknown definition.

SHELBY (English) Estate on a ledge. Shelby is most commonly thought of as a name for boys and as a last name,

but was one of the hottest names in the mid-'90s for baby girls. Variations: *Shelbee, Shelbey, Shellby.*

SHELLEY (English) Meadow on a ledge. Variations: *Shellee, Shelli, Shellie, Shelly.*

SIBYL (Greek) Seer, oracle. Variations: *Sibbell, Sibel, Sibell, Sibella, Sibelle, Sibila, Sibyll, Sibylla, Sybel, Sybella, Sybelle, Sybil, Sybill, Sybilla, Sybille, Sybyl.*

SIERRA (English) Mountain. Variation: *Siera.*

SIGOURNEY (English) Unknown definition.

SIMONE (French) God listens. Feminine version of Simon. Variations: *Simona, Simonetta, Simonette, Simonia, Simonina, Symona, Symone.*

SKYLER (Dutch) Shelter. Variations: *Schuyler, Skye.*

SOPHIA (Greek) Wisdom. Sophia and its close relation Sophie have both zoomed onto the top 10 list in the United States and Great Britain. Sophie holds a slight edge over Sophia in popularity. Variations: *Sofi, Sofia, Soficita, Sofka, Sofya, Sophey, Sophie, Sophy, Zofe, Zofia, Zofie, Zofka, Zosha, Zosia.*

STEPHANIE (English) Crown. Feminine version of Stephen. Stephanie is turning into one of those perennially popular names. Variations: *Stefania, Stefanie, Steffi, Stepania, Stepanie, Stephana, Stephanine, Stephannie, Stephena, Stephene, Stepheney, Stephenie, Stephine, Stephne, Stephney, Stevana, Stevena, Stevey, Stevi, Stevie.*

SUMI (Japanese) Clear.

SUSAN (Hebrew) Lily. Variations: *Susann, Susanna, Susannah, Susanne, Susetta, Susette, Susi, Susie, Susy,*

Suzan, Suzane, Suzanna, Suzannah, Suzanne, Suzetta, Suzette, Suzi, Suzie, Suzy, Zsa Zsa, Zusa, Zuza.

SUZUKI (Japanese) Little bell tree. Variations: *Suzue, Suzuko.*

SVETLANA (Czech) Star. Variations: *Svetla, Svetlanka, Svetluse, Svetluvska.*

SYDNEY (French) Feminine version of Sidney. Saint Denis. Variations: *Sydnie, Sydny.*

SYLVIA (Latin) From the forest. Variations: *Silvana, Silvia, Silvianne, Silvie, Sylva, Sylvana, Sylvanna, Sylvee, Sylvie.*

SYONA (Hindu) Happy.

SYREETA (Arabic) Companion.

TABITHA (English) Gazelle. Variations: *Tabatha, Tabbitha, Tabby, Tabetha, Tabotha, Tabytha.*

TALIA (Hebrew) Dew. In the Old Testament, Talia was the name of one of the angels who escorted the Sun from Dawn to Dusk. Variations: *Talie, Talley, Tallie, Tally, Talora, Talya, Thalie, Thalya.*

TALLULAH (Native American: Choctaw) Leaping water. Variations: *Tallula, Talula, Talulah, Talulla*.

TARA (Irish) Hill. The name of the estate in *Gone with the Wind* seems to have served as the catalyst for the increasing presence of this name in the United States and in England. Variations: *Tarah, Taran, Tareena, Tarena, Tarin, Tarina, Tarra, Tarrah, Tarren, Tarryn, Taryn, Taryna, Teryn*.

TASHA (Russian) Christmas. Diminutive of Natasha. Variations: *Tashina, Tashka, Tasia*.

TASHANEE (African-American) Unknown definition.

TATIANA (Russian) Ancient Slavic king. Feminine version of Tatius. Variations: *Latonya, Tahnya, Tana, Tania, Tanis, Tanka, Tannia, Tannis, Tarnia, Tarny, Tata, Tatianna, Tatyana, Tatyanna, Tonia, Tonya, Tonyah*.

TAYLOR (English) Tailor. Variations: *Tailor, Talor, Tayler*.

TEMPEST (French) Storm.

TERESA (Greek) Harvest. Teresa and all of its variations are wonderfully feminine names that are as timely today as they were back in the '60s, when they first started to become popular in the United States. Variations: *Terasa,*

Teree, Terese, Teresia, Teresina, Teresita, Teressa, Teri, Terie, Terise, Terrasa, Terresa, Terresia, Terri, Terrie, Terrise, Terry, Terrya, Tersa, Terza, Tess, Tessa, Tessie, Tessy, Theresa, Therese, Theressa, Thereza, Thersa, Thersea.

TESSA (Polish) Beloved by God. Variations: *Tess, Tessia, Tessie.*

THEODORA (Greek) Gift of God. Feminine version of Theodore. Theodora has only begun to catch on, so look for more girls with this name over the next 10 to 15 years. Variations: *Teddy, Teodora, Theadora, Theda, Theodosia.*

TIFFANY (Greek) God's appearance. Modern version of Theophania. As the '80s went, so did certain baby names, and Tiffany was one of these. Today, the name is starting to fall out of fashion. Variations: *Tifani, Tiff, Tiffaney, Tiffani, Tiffanie, Tiffiney, Tiffini, Tiffney, Tiffy.*

TOVAH (Hebrew) Pleasant. Variations: *Toba, Tobit, Tova, Tovat, Tovit.*

TRACY (English) Summer. Variation of Teresa. Tracy was one of the more popular gender-neutral names back in the '60s when it was in the middle of its transition from boys' name to girls' name. Variations: *Trace, Tracee, Tracey, Traci, Tracie, Trasey, Treacy, Treesy.*

TRICIA (English) Noble. Feminine version of Patrick. Variations: *Treasha, Trichia, Trish, Trisha.*

TRIXIE (English) She brings happiness. Variation of Beatrice. Variations: *Trix, Trixi, Trixy.*

TWYLA (African-American) Newly created. Variations: *Twila, Twylla.*

TYLER (English) Last name.

UMA (Hindu) Flax.

URANIA (Greek) Heavenly. Variations: *Urainia, Uraniya, Uranya.*

URSULA (Latin) Little female bear. Variations: *Ursala, Ursella, Ursola, Ursule, Ursulina, Ursuline.*

VALERIE (Latin) Strong. A popular name during the Roman Empire, Valerie tends to be underused today. Variations: *Val, Valaree, Valarey, Valaria, Valarie, Vale, Valeree, Valeria, Valeriana, Valery, Vallarie, Valleree, Vallerie, Valli, Vallie, Vally.*

VANESSA (Greek) Butterflies. Variations: *Vanesa, Vanesse, Vania, Vanna, Vannessa, Venesa, Venessa.*

VANNA (Cambodian) Golden.

VASHTI (Persian) Beautiful.

VENETTA (English) Newly created. Variations: *Veneta, Venette.*

VENUS (Latin) Roman goddess of love. Variations: *Venise, Vennice, Venusa, Venusina.*

VERA (Slavic) Faith. Vera was at its height in both the United States and Britain during the flapper days of the '20s. Variations: *Veera, Veira, Verasha, Viera.*

VERONICA (Latin) True image. Variations: *Veranique, Vernice, Veron, Verona, Verone, Veronice, Veronicka, Veronika, Veronike, Veroniqua, Veronique.*

VICTORIA (Latin) Roman goddess of victory. Victoria is a name that has had a number of spurts in popularity since the days of the early Roman Empire, when it was one of the most frequently bestowed names for girls. Variations: *Torey, Tori, Toria, Torie, Torrey, Torri, Torrie, Torrye, Tory, Vicki, Vickie, Vicky, Victoriana, Victorina, Victorine, Victory, Vikki, Vikky, Vitoria, Vittoria.*

VIOLET (Latin) Violet. Variations: *Viola, Violetta, Violette.*

VIRGINIA (Latin) Virgin. Variations: *Vergie, Virgy, Virginie, Vegenia, Virginai, Virgena, Virgene.*

VIVIAN (Latin) Full of life. Actress Vivien Leigh was responsible for the name's first burst of popularity in the United States in the '40s. Variations: *Viv, Viva, Viveca, Vivecka, Viveka, Vivia, Viviana, Viviane, Vivianna, Vivianne, Vivie, Vivien, Vivienne.*

WALLIS (English) One from Wales. Feminine version of Wallace. Variations: *Wallie, Walliss, Wally, Wallys.*

WASHI (Japanese) Eagle.

WENDY (English) Wendy first appeared as the name of a character in the novel, *Peter Pan*. Variations: *Wenda, Wendee, Wendey, Wendi, Wendie, Wendye, Windy.*

WHITLEY (English) White field.

WHITNEY (English) White island. Variations: *Whitnee, Whitnie, Whitny, Whittney.*

WHOOPI (French) Unknown definition.

WILHELMINA (German) Feminine version of William, Will + helmet. Variations: *Wiletta, Wilette, Wilhelmine, Willa, Willamina, Williamina.*

WILMA (German) Feminine version of William, Will + helmet. Variations: *Wilmette, Wilmina, Wylma.*

WINIFRED (Welsh) Holy peace. Winifred is a pretty name that is both delicate and powerful. Variations: *Win,*

Winifrede, Winifride, Winifryde, Winne, Winni, Winnie, Winny, Wyn, Wynn.

WINTER (English) Winter.

WYNN (Welsh) Fair, white. Variations: *Winne, Wynne.*

WYNONAH (Native American) First-born. Variations: *Wenona, Wenonah, Winona, Winonah, Wynnona.*

XANTHIPPE (Greek) Wife of Socrates.

XAVIERA (English) New house. Feminine version of Xavier. The name Xaviera started out as the name of a saint from the sixteenth century. Variations: *Xavier, Xavyera.*

XENIA (Greek) Hospitable. Variations: *Xeenia, Xena.*

XIANG (Chinese) Fragrant.

XIAO-XING (Chinese) Morning star.

YAKI (Japanese) Snow. Variations: *Yukie, Yukika, Yukiko.*

YASMINE (Arabic) Flower. Though Jasmin, the name from which Yasmine is derived, is the more well-known variation of this name, Yasmine is likely to become more popular in time, simply because many parents will want to put their unique spin on what is becoming a relatively popular name. Variations: *Yasmeen, Yasmeena, Yasmena, Yasmene, Yasmin, Yasmina.*

YASU (Japanese) Calm. Variations: *Yasuko, Yasuyo.*

YEHUDIT (Hebrew) God will be praised. Variations: *Yudi, Yudit, Yudita, Yuta, Yutke.*

YELENA (Russian) Light. Variation of Helen. Variation: *Yalena.*

YENTA (Hebrew) Ruler at home. Variations: *Yente, Yentel, Yentele, Yentil.*

YETTA (English) Ruler at home. Feminine diminutive version of Henry. Variation: *Yette.*

YOKO (Japanese) Child of the ocean.

YOLANDA (Greek) Purple flower. Yolanda first appeared as the name of a saint in thirteenth-century Spain, and later belonged to Hungarian royalty. Though some parents might feel the name is dated and too unusual to use today, it's clear that others disagree. Variations: *Eolanda, Eolande, Iolanda, Iolande, Yalanda, Yalinda, Yalonda, Yola, Yoland, Yolande, Yolane, Yolette, Yoli, Yolonda, Yulanda.*

YORI (Japanese) Honest.

YOSHIKO (Japanese) Quiet. Variations: *Yoshi, Yoshie, Yoshiyo.*

YOUNG-SOON (Korean) Tender flower.

YVETTE (French) Arrow's bow.

YVONNE (French) Yew wood. Variations: *Yvetta, Yvette, Yvone.*